"This will be of fine service for you, you bag of the scum. I am sure you will not mind that I remove your manhoods and leave them out on the dessert flour for your aunts to eat."

MAY 2012
ISSUE 0

CHOP

CONTENTS:

Covert art: David Barnes
Interior art: Amber Skowronski

Brian Harris, Editor & Publisher
Timothy Paxton, Editor & Lay Out/Design

EDITORIAL ...

To publish a zine, or remain digital: that is the question. While so many would simply take the path of least resistance, remain online and simply slap "Zine" on their blog, a few trashphiles and myself yearned to hold a real deal fanzine in our hairy palms and read about the films we hoard so dear. Downloading something to your phone, or even reading it on a desk/laptop, can be convenient, especially when you're allergic to books, but nothing quite compares to a few pieces of stapled paper filled with the kind of passion only cinema geeks possess. We knew what had to be done, we just had to figure out what to call it and what to write about.

WENG'S CHOP was initially supposed to be a one-shot deal but the mad creativity that went into this issue was so electrifying I decided to make it a quarterly affair. I mean, I don't know about some of you out there but I fucking hate finishing an insanely entertaining book/comic only to discover it's a one-time deal and the story won't be continued! Nuts to that, I say! The stable of ultra-talented contributors/sleazehounds will, cinema gods willing, be back again for the next orgy 'round and you'll probably see the following installment sometime around June 2012. Hell, we may even whip up a goddamn digital copy just for the Kindle junkies out there. We'll see, it's all about demand, ya know?

Without the help of gentleman, scholar and zine legend Tim "Monster!" Paxton, this endeavor may have ended up drawn out with fecal matter mixed with tears of shame and held together with a few strategically placed boogers. Not only has he contributed to the awesome material but he skillfully laid this behemoth out, putting us (in my humble opinion) on a completely different plain of cool. A zine isn't worth shit without dedicated contributors and WENG'S CHOP has got those baby, by the boatload! After reading the articles and reviews in this issue, please seek out the writers and check out their websites, they're the best of the best when it comes to trash cinema. You won't be disappointed.

I hope you enjoy yourselves. See you in a few months!

Humpingly Yours,   Brian Harris
WildsideCinema.com

...CONTRIBUTORS

Bennie Woodell is a filmmaker born and raised in Chicago, now living the dream in LA. Hong Kong cinema is his passion, looking up to Wong Kar-Wai, Chang Cheh, and Johnnie To as his main inspirations. Woodell has directed four feature films. His latest film, **THE SAD CAFE**, an homage to Hong Kong cinema, recently won Best Drama Feature at the Action On Film Festival in Pasadena, California. His second feature film, **FAST ZOMBIES WITH GUNS**, was recently released nationwide in Family Video stores by Chemical Burn Entertainment, who also distributed his third feature, **DEATH ANGEL DECEMBER: VENGEANCE KILL**. Woodell's favorite film is **ASHES OF TIME**, and thinks the best acting duo is Tony Leung Chiu-Wai and Maggie Cheung. For more information on Woodell and his films, please visit jianghuproductions.net

Dan Taylor has been writing about junk culture and fringe media since his zine Exploitation Retrospect debuted in 1986. 26 years later the publication is still going strong as a website, blog and -- yes -- a resurrected print edition. Check it all out at Dantenet.com, EROnline.blogspot.com or Facebook.com/ExploitationRetrospect.

David Zuzelo is a full time father, part time Joe D'Amato Porn Excavator and non-stop Media Mangler. He has been writing about stuff for over a decade online and you can peek into his slightly unhinged brain by pointing your webmind at David-Z.blogspot.com. Print oriented readers can pick up his co-authored book on Italian action cinema, TOUGH TO KILL-THE ITALIAN ACTION EXPLOSION or just try and find some of his comics work in ZOMBIE TERRORS or A.K.A. if you dare! Lamberto is his favorite Bava.

Jason Meredith is an Englishman raised on Dr. Who, Hammer Horror and Ray Harryhausen flicks. He resides in Sweden, where he works as an executive TV producer and freelance movie journalist. Graduated from the University of BVFM (Bootleg Videos & Fangoria Magazine), he runs Cinezilla, his blog where he tries to put his past film studies to use, by applying classic storytelling rules, and new ones specific to the genre, to the horror genre. A genre he claims is amongst the hardest to master. He stacks movies at his home in Stockholm, where he lives with his family, and prefers to play vinyl at night whilst he's writing.

Joachim Andersson is a practicing rubbermonsterfetishist and worshiper of 70s exploitation (preferably Spanish horror smut). While not watching movies he dabbles in electronic music (music featured in a danish torture porn flick and released

a dark ambient album in 2007 that included a tribute piece to Jesus Franco's lovely **OASIS OF THE ZOMBIES**). Buys more movies than he watches and feels somewhat uncomfortable with writing about himself in third person. Visit his blog at http://rubbermonsterfetishism.blogspot.com

Mike Haushalter is a lifelong film fan. He formed an anime club, Moonlight Ramblers, in 1991, and he remains president for life. When that group disbanded in 1997, he and pal Matt Gilligan started up a review and interview 'zine called Secret Scroll Digest that ran until 2005. He has worked as firearms wrangler and craft services on several Happy Cloud Pictures productions, giving him insight into life behind the camera that many film reviewers lack. His greatest film disappointment is the time his grandma promised to take him to **STAR WARS**, but they saw **CLOSE ENCOUNTERS OF THE THIRD KIND** instead.

Phillip Escott is a British movie lover with a boner for not just the finest trash, but the best art house. Basically he likes anything that shows boobies. When he's not admiring naked bodies he's attempting to make films. He urges/will blow you if you come and watch his 'films'. You can reach Phill through www.facebook.com/441films

Tim Paxton is a life-long hermit with a very understanding girlfriend. In eons past he was editor and founder of numerous faznines, and only recently sold his soul to the Old Ones for another chance to reach out and be one with humanity.

Betsy Burger was born in a hospital to creative types in 1965. In the 1990s, she wrote for Something Weird Video, and edited Highball Magazine for Kronos Productions. Betsy lives in Sheffield Lake, Ohio with her impossibly wonderful family, where she watches television and practices mediocre housekeeping. She has no favorite movie, color, or food.

Brian Harris: see editorial.

Amber Skowronski is an Illustrator and Special Effects Artist living in Los Angeles. http://ninjasquid.blogspot.com/

David Barnes has his own line of comics and also creates vintage ''grindhouse '' t-shirts. **His work can be seen at zid3ya@yahoo.com and myspace.com@paramere.**

IS EXPLOITATION CINEMA RIGHT FOR ME?

WRITTEN BY BRIAN HARRIS

Over the years I've crossed paths with many people interested in becoming exploitation/cult cinema fans, as if one could "choose" to be such a way, and I've done my best to point them in the direction of beginner fare before leading them into the real ugliness. A few (very few) have remaained, the rest faded away when they realized that it isn't at all the campy fun of MST3K or their local horror host. Certainly exploitation and cult cinema can be campy fun but, generally speaking, it's sleazy and offensive; the lowest common denominator served up on a nudie girl plate by a horny black girl named Nubia. It stinks, it's sticky and ugly, and it grates on your ears like the sound of a million chalk boards being clawed at. You don't become a fan of exploitation cinema for the "fun" of it, you become one because that screeching sound of abused chalk boards is like sweet music to your foul little ears. We may not look like whacked-out mental patients or skeevy perverts but, trust me, there's a wee bit of both in each and every exploitation fan.

It takes a special kind of lowlife to love what we love.

Are you that special kinda lowlife? Well, are you capable of being strongly against racism yet fully capable of enjoying films in which the words nigger, spic, chink, honky, cracker, coon, wap, guinea, greaseball, midget, mick and paddy are used? Are you strongly against the abuse of women, and rape specifically, yet unfazed (or even entertained) by rape fantasy and rape/revenge cinema? When somebody says "little people," do you automatically think fondly of **RUNAWAY MIDGET** and **THE SINFUL DWARF**? Does the thought of the Third Reich's attempted genocide of the Jewish people sicken you, while films featuring debaucherous Nazi-on-Jewess orgies put a smile on your face? Are you laughing at my absurd and patently offensive and unacceptable line of questioning?

You just might be the special kind of lowlife it takes to be an exploitation fan.

Like any fan of cinema, exploitation fans know how to separate fantasy from reality. We know right from

wrong. Nobody watches **THE NEVERENDING STORY** and waits on a cliff for Falkor to fly by nor would anybody watch **TERMINATOR** and then attack a toaster with a shotgun in anticipation of the truck-turner coming conflagration between man and machine. We're no different. Outrageous examples, sure, but you get the picture. If horror is the heavy metal of cinema, exploitation is gangsta rap, death metal and Cantopop all rolled into one smelly, Wild Turkey-sippin', white girl-slappin', long dick-havin', midget pimp named Chow-Ming Rodriguez.

Is exploitation cinema right for you? You'll never know until you check it out but keep in mind, whether you like it or you do not, you're no better or worse a person for it. You won't go to Hell. It won't make you a racist. You won't hate or mistreat women. You won't murder or rape anybody. You won't even spiral into drug abuse and end up blowing stiff donkey junk in seedy Mexican porno circuses to pay your rent like I did. Don't knock it, donkeys taste like chicken.

Honestly I can't tell you whether exploitation cinema is right for you, only you can do that. Take a moment though and reflect on what it really means to be entertained and whether your politics or real-life tragedies may get in the way of that. You might be surprised and find you love it. Or not. Bitch.

(Reprinted from WildsideCinema.com)

www.WILDSIDECINEMA.COM

THE REVIEWS...

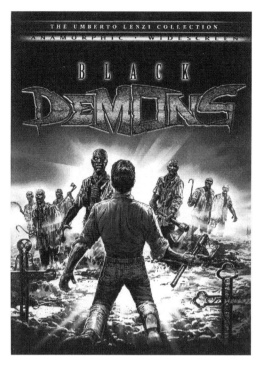

THE UMBERTO LENZI COLLECTION
ANAMORPHIC · WIDESCREEN
BLACK DEMONS

ANNO 2053-LA GRANDE FUGA

Vidmark Entertainment / 1991
Reviewed by Brian Harris

After bounty hunter Harry Stark (Michael Ironside) nabs wanted murderer Reno (Vanity) it looks as though her days of running from the law have come to an end, but that couldn't be further from the truth. Forced aboard a rickety passenger transport bound for Neon City, Reno, her hardened captor and a small group of travelers must face the perils of a wasteland fraught with danger and death. If cycle-riding scavenger tribes don't get you, the noxious gases and deadly rays from the sun will. Welcome to Xander's utopia and 2053!

Say what you will about this being nothing more than a Mad Max rip-off, **ANNO 2053 - LA GRANDE FUGA** is still worth checking out as it offers up an interesting low budget post-nuke scenario with engaging, oddball characters including the imposing transport driver Bulk (Lyle Alzado), skittish salesman of death Dickie Devine (played by Richard Sanders of "WKRP in Cincinnati") and the sheltered-to-a-fault, high society girl Twink Talaman (Juliey Landau). The acting from all involved, especially Ironside's cuke-cool Stark, was exactly what

you'd expect from a low budget sci-fi affair, I mean nobody was going to win any awards for their roles but entertainment is entertainment, right? The real shame of this production was the passing of legendary sports icon, and surprisingly talented actor, Lyle Alzado (Destroyer) not long after from brain cancer.

The film's shooting locations ranged from slushy snow to sand and random patches of grass, creating this downright nasty, barely habitable look. When you see an actor's breath while he's delivering his lines, you know damn well it really was cold, wherever they were! The production was filmed in both California and Utah so, I'm assuming, the thawing tundra was Utah and the desert areas were California, both great choices. Sure, a few painted backgrounds of smoldering ruins may have helped give this production a bit more authenticity but it still ends up working despite its meager offerings.

ANNO 2053 - LA GRANDE FUGA was an impressive, well-written post-nuke action/drama and I'll be damned if throwing in the stunning Vanity didn't kick this up a notch for me. If she'd been nude...if she'd only been nude. If your apocalyptic cinema must include face-painted, dirt bike riding marauders, incurable (and gory) diseases and a glimmer of hope for mankind, this just might be your lucky day. It's a shame director Monte Markham went on to direct a few "Baywatch" episodes instead of making more films like this. Seek this one out, if you can find it, and add it to your collection.

BLACK DEMONS

Media Blasters / 1991
Reviewed by Phillip Escott

Umberto Lenzi holds a special place in my heart. He knows exactly what he's making, much like his fellow countryman Bruno Mattei, glorified trash cinema that pleases the basest needs of my cerebral cortex. Be it Gialli movies, haunted house movies or zombie flicks Lenzi delivers the goods time and time again; that's not to say all his films are actually good in any respectful form, far from it, his is the cinema of bad taste done right. **BLACK DEMONS** however, would see him take this trash cinema to its limit.

Three white tourists are enjoying their time in Brazil, soaking up the sun and enjoying its culture, until one of them decides to dabble in Macumba and ends up getting his dumbass possessed. If that wasn't trouble enough for the group he goes and raises the souls of six black slaves who are looking to get some righteous payback on whitey! Now, I find the premise of black slaves coming back to take revenge on white people a great one and in the right hands that could produce a fine horror film; but it's in Umberto's hands and it comes across as more than a little racist. The fun factor here comes from the casts' terrible,

terrible acting and Lenzi's complete mishandling of the material. The political incorrectness only adds to the film's charms as nothing about this film is competently carried out.

The 'Demons' are actually zombies, it's made in the 90s but feels very much a product of the 80s and the dialogue and delivery are masterworks in how not to be done. Watch, learn and be amazed at the absurdity. Those who thought Lenzi couldn't make a more fucked up zombie film than **NIGHTMARE CITY**, check this out. It's nowhere near the greatness of his first attempt at the living dead but it sure as shit manages to out trash it; your brain will hurt, your eyes and ears too but you know what? It's all worth it just to say you've managed to sit through it all.

BODY PUZZLE

Raro Video / 1992
Reviewed by Dan Taylor

Bava! Garko! Blanc!

Had **BODY PUZZLE** been made in 1970, those names plastered above the title may have led to the flick being remembered more fondly than it is. Unfortunately, the late-to-the-game thriller landed on screens circa 1992 and features the directorial flourishes of underappreciated Bava offspring Lamberto with spaghetti western vet Gianni Garko in the thankless role of "Police Chief" while the GILFy Erica Blanc turns up for just a couple scenes as a divorced psychiatrist who is "crazy about tennis".

But I'm getting ahead of myself.

It's been a tough day for Tracy (played by Joanna Pacula and her signature eyebrows), a lovely widow whose husband Abe died in a tragic motorcycle accident. Not only have her hubbie's remains been disinterred and stolen from the cemetery, but a maniac has also hacked a candy store manager to death and left the victim's severed ear in her fridge. Tough but frazzled cop Mike Livitt (Tomas Arana) arrives on the scene and begins his investigation amidst a growing list of body parts and victims. The crazed killer – who grooves on the classical hit "Night on Bald Mountain" as he stalks and slashes his prey – hacks hands, gouges eyes and even slices off what we're told is "not a finger" in one of the film's many moments of black comedy.

Between bedding the frightened widow (and her eyebrows) and dealing with a boss more concerned with covering his own ass the detective must put together the pieces of Abe's shadowy double-life and track down the killer before it's too late. To reveal any more of **BODY PUZZLE**'s convoluted plot would ruin the surprises the filmmakers have in store though I inadvertently spoiled one piece of the film's cryptic plotline for myself when I was checking on a cast member via IMDB. Doh!

Overly-plotted to the point of occasionally being nonsensical, the script spends the first two-thirds of its running time lumping plot points upon plot points upon red herrings. A bit too late in the game for my taste Bava embraces the outrageousness of the storyline, finally reveling in cliché genre tropes (like the sandwich eating coroner) and having characters pop out of freezers, hack off wieners and provide various funhouse shocks as the killer's motives come to light. Sorta.

In a reversal of the trend for such films the flick was trimmed of violence for its Italian release (where it was re-titled Misteria) yet kept its run-of-the-mill gore for its American debut, where it faded into semi-obscurity. It's unfortunate that **BODY PUZZLE** chooses to tread such a fine line between its bid for mainstream acceptance and off-the-wall black comedy as the first hour is neither sleazy enough to appeal to trash hounds nor packs the thrills to grab fans who might be attracted to its mystery elements. By the time Tracy is gasping "it was imported beer!" and Livitt is making ill-timed references to keeping "eyes open" even the most hardened Eurotrash fan may have lost interest.

The English dub is good and the performances by Pacula and Arana are solid if uninspired, though I'd admittedly watch another Mike Livitt adventure had they made one. Extras are non-existent but the real bonus is getting to see genre vets Garko, Blanc and Giovanni Lombardo Radice (aka John Morghen) grace the screen again, albeit in brief supporting roles.

Light years away from his stellar work with **DEMONS**, Baby Bava's **BODY PUZZLE** makes for an interesting curio from the end of the Giallo era that ends up being more frustrating than it is entertaining.

BOHACHI BUSHIDO: CODE OF THE FORGOTTEN EIGHT

(Bôhachi Bushidô: Poruno Jidaigeki)
Discotek Media / 1973
Review by Joachim Andersson

Japan, I love you! I bow down to the glory that is **BOHACHI BUSHIDO** aka *Poruno Jidaigeki*. It's like there is a Heaven and I've been given a glimpse of the wonderful light and its warmth still glows within me!

No, I have not gone religious, I've just watched Teruo Ishii's supreme blend of boobs and violence that is **BOHACHI BUSHIDO: CODE OF THE FORGOTTEN EIGHT**. Movies like this always try to balance on a small thread but they either rely too much

not really care. He is a bad-ass whose motto is "To die is Hell, but to live is also Hell" and has a bodyguard consisting of five naked women. Ah, don't we all want to be just like Shino.

Yes, this is Entertainment with a capital E. Sure, the plot is mainly an excuse to show nudity and graphic violence but it is still treated 100 percent seriously by Teruo Ishii, a director whose output is not like anything else in the same period. Every shot is treated like a painting, stylish and beautiful and this is what makes the movie unique and keeps it from being just another Pinku violence piece. The 81 minutes run by faster than lightning and you kind of wish that the movie was several hours longer. There is so much fun stuff to watch, tons of nudity and severed body parts. If you have any interest in Japanese exploitation, you must own this. And worship it.

THE BURNING MOON

Intervision /1997
Reviewed by Brian Harris

Finally receiving an official release thru Severin Films' Intervision sub-label, Olaf Ittenbach's nasty little cult film **THE BURNING MOON** sees DVD, reaching the gore faithful and oddity collector alike. Whether you're a rabid Ittenbach fan, a German underground horror junkie or simply looking for something outside the norm to watch, Ittenbach's gruesome anthology is sure to hit the spot. Containing two stories and a wrap-around, **THE BURNING MOON** introduces us to a drugged-out loser as he tells his "bitch" of a little sister two terrifying tales of bloodshed and dismemberment.

"Julia's Love" - Julia doesn't seem to have much luck with men but she's got a hot date lined up for dinner and he's quite the catch. Too bad she has no idea he's an escaped lunatic and a raging psychopath with head-lopping, arm-severing and leg-loosening on his agenda! Talk about a nightmare ex!

"The Purity" - A village priest with a penchant for vicious rape and Satanic rituals befriends a local simpleton being accused of crimes the holy man committed! When the shit hits the fan and the villagers make their move to punish the innocent man, the priest takes sinister steps to help the simpleton avenge his own murder.

It would be a bit of a stretch to insist **THE BURNING MOON** is a horror classic, that's simply not the case, but it's not at all hard to see why this is such a sought after film by collectors of German gore and horror either; it's filled with cheesy, bloody mayhem and a truly chilling sequence featuring Ittenbach's interpretation of Hell. The latter is guaranteed to impress even the most jaded of fan. Despite the film's obvious budgetary restrictions, there are some impressive gore set-pieces, something no respectable German horror film can do without. Like most

on violence (eh. as if there can be too much violence in a movie) or too much sex, which frankly tends to be a bit boring after a while. This movie, however, is truly the perfect mix of nipples and sliced off ears that exists in this day. Based on a manga by the creators of Lone Wolf and Cub (which most likely is even more sick and violent than the movie. Thank you Japan.), the movie stars Tetsuro Tanba (You've all seen him as Tiger Tanaka in the Bond movie **YOU ONLY LIVE TWICE**) as Shino, the coldest Ronin ever, a guy that makes Itto Ogami seem like Jim Carrey. After slaughtering a number of officers in a stylized fight on a bridge, he is taken in by the Clan Of The Forgotten Eight, a group that takes its name from the fact that they've lost the way to feel basic emotions like shame, guilt and conscience. They run a prostitution racket and want Shino to clean out the other groups while under their protection. Of course, all of this is a diabolical plot by the leader of the clan who intends to dispose of Shino as soon as he no longer is needed but Shino does

SOV affairs, it suffers miserably from terrible acting and an overall sense of having "been here, done this" with the story itself. Having rumored to of been made in 1992, folks familiar with this style of early underground shot-on-video filmmaking will probably be accustomed to acting and script issues. Those of you that are not though, you may want to procure a copy from a friend to view before running out and purchasing.

Love it or hate it, if you're not laughing midway thru the awkward "gang" fight in the beginning of this film, you're one hard-hearted S.O.B.

CAVE OF THE SHARKS

(Bermude: La Fossa Maledetta)
European Trash Cinema / 1978
Reviewed by Joachim Andersson

As many horror movie fans out there, I was a proud owner of Phil Hardy's giant tome of snobby movie reviews, The Encyclopedia of Horror Movies. Many days were spent memorizing the damn thing and still today there are movies in it that I have never seen, longing for a nice DVD. One of those movies was Tonino Ricci's *Bermude: La Fossa Maledetta* aka **CAVE OF THE SHARKS**, a rather odd movie that has a fun and intriguing concept, but a low budget that hampers the fun a bit. Still, as corny exploitation this works just fine.

Hunky Andrés Garcia plays Andres Montoya, a fisherman that was lost at sea for six months, not even having any recollection of where he has been. He gets together with his old girlfriend (Janet Ågren), causing friction with his brother who is in love with her but really, this doesn't have anything to do with the plot. Andres is hired by an American businessman (Arthur Kennedy) to recover valuables from an airplane that supposedly sunk in the Bermuda Triangle. When he and a friend go on a dive they discover a mysterious cave full of sleeping sharks, and Andres starts to get flashbacks on what may have happened to him earlier. When the American double-crosses them, even weirder things start to happen. His friend is sucked into some sort of underwater portal; there is a shitload of really poor underwater miniatures and the sleeping sharks wake up. We get a rather cool sequence when our hero tries to make it back to his boat by feeding the sharks with the bodies of the American henchmen.

No, nothing really makes any sense. The Bermuda Triangle seems to be about a kilometer outside whatever tourist resort Tonino Ricci chose to film this at (you see the shore all the time), there is a long sequence where a bunch of hippies on a boat stare at a weird doll that starts to ooze blood through its mouth, to which all of them commit suicide by drowning (a rather atmospheric sequence that really doesn't have anything to do with the rest of

the movie) and then there are those fish tank miniatures... But the story in itself is fairly intriguing, the dreamlike visuals are atmospheric (thanks to Stelvio Cipriani's score full of its bleeps and bloops) and although the miniatures are awful, they do bring a certain weird something into the story as long as you are in the right mood. This isn't a **JAWS** clone, it is a weird sci-fi movie with sharks and although nothing really gels into a coherent experience, it is still weird enough to warrant a watch.

THE EXTERMINATOR

Synapse Films / 1980
Reviewed by Dan Taylor

"It didn't matter whether it was right or wrong. I just did it."

I'd be lying if I said that I was capable of any kind of critical analysis when it comes to James Glickenhaus' 1980 vigilante masterpiece **THE EXTERMINATOR**. It belongs to that rarified group of flicks that made up my initial trip to the rental store in the mid-80s when I got my first VCR. And, like **THE TEXAS CHAIN SAW MASSACRE, BLOODSUCKING FREAKS** and **THE EVIL DEAD** watching it brings a huge, high school trashhound's smile to my face.

Inspired by a real-life crime that left a university professor paralyzed, the $2 million flick would go on to gross $35 million worldwide thanks to its incomparable blend of action, location Times Square sleazery, snappy pacing and dark humor. Like a men's adventure novel come to life, the flick promises exactly what it delivers: a dude with a flamethrower making some scumbags pay.

An impressive **APOCALYPSE NOW**-inspired open featuring a memorable Stan Winston-created beheading introduces us to John Eastland (TV vet Robert Ginty cast in the role after Joseph Bottoms was sacked) and Michael Jefferson (Steve James), who escape from their captors amidst a hail of bullets and flaming Viet Cong. Back home in NYC, the two work the docks at the food terminals, hauling cases of beer and sides of beef while mobsters squeeze cash from the owner and thugs treat the stalls like their personal vending machine.

When the pair run afoul of The Ghetto Ghouls (my favorite on-screen gang next to The Baseball Furies), the gang members exact their revenge on Jefferson and leave the hulking father of two paralyzed, "possibly for the rest of his life". Roused into action by the attack on his best friend, Eastland hauls out his 'Nam gear – and a trusty flamethrower – to take down the Ghouls, as well as any other thugs, perverts and purse snatchers that cross his path.

Glickenhaus makes very few missteps in this, his second feature effort. The director never bores us with scenes of

The Exterminator driving anywhere or doing anything that doesn't advance the plot. Even when he picks up a hooker in Times Square he sets aside his manly needs after seeing the scars left behind when some chicken hawk and a sleazebag politician (from New Jersey, 'natch) burned her titties. The only scenes that feel superfluous feature Dalton, a NYC cop and the Brit doctor he's bedding. Played, respectively, by Christopher George and Samantha Egger, the pair gives the flick what little name recognition it had at the time of its release.

Sure, the ending feels a bit rushed and anti-climactic and no matter how many times I see it I still expect Dalton and The Exterminator to battle the shadowy forces from our nation's capital. But it's hard to argue with a flick that features everything from beheadings and immolation to torture via flamethrower and giant meat grinder.

The Synapse Films combo pack features both a Blu-Ray and standard DVD with a slightly gorier "unrated director's cut" restored from original vault materials. Bonus features include a commentary track from the director as well as the red band theatrical trailer and a collection of vintage TV spots.

It's too bad the collection couldn't also include the inferior 1984 sequel **THE EXTERMINATOR 2** featuring Ginty's return as The Exterminator. The Cannon-financed flick features the vigilante driving an armored garbage truck while he battles a gang led by the sinister X (Mario Van Peebles). The flick has never been released on DVD but I strongly encourage fans of either film in the series to pick up SCREEM #23 for the excellent article "The Exterminator Burns Its Way to Blu-Ray" by Bronson's Loose author Paul Talbot.

FATHER'S DAY

Astron-6 & Troma Entertainment / 2011
Reviewed by Brian Harris

Some out there may disagree with me on this but, in my opinion, Troma really seemed to of lost their creative spark. As a matter of fact, up until the release of their wonderfully raunchy **POULTRYGEIST: NIGHT OF THE CHICKEN DEAD**, I was positive they would close their doors forever. Thankfully the chicken flick appeared to be quite successful and they lived to fight, and entertain, another day.

Enter the Canadian quintet known as Astron-6 and their unique brand of gonzo, 80s-style, late night, made-for-television, move-of-the-week filmmaking and their absurdly original, and outrageously offensive, feature film, **FATHER'S DAY**. What **POULTRYGEIST: NIGHT OF THE CHICKEN DEAD** did for Troma in '07/'08, **FATHER'S DAY** has been doing for them in '11/'12; essentially putting them back on the genre cinema radar.

When the father-raping psycho-killer Chris Fuchman turns up on the streets once again, to ply his poopy and gruesome trade, the Roman Catholic Church calls on the only man capable of doing the job right, a grizzled ex-con with a shady past named Ahab. He won't be alone in this holiest of assignments though, he's joined by male prostitute Twink and a young priest named Father John Sullivan. Together the men will face the sickest depravities, and even Hell itself, in order to save Ahab's sister and foil Fuchman's unholy plan to rule the world!

Doesn't sound nearly as twisted on paper as it actually is on the big screen but, trust me on this, **FATHER'S DAY** is seriously fucked up. It's oozing oodles of ass-rape, incest, suicide, fellatio, murder, gore up the ass (pun intended) and genuine comedy; Astron-6 went toe-to-toe, mano-a-mano with good taste and beat it senseless. While so many others are opting for the faux exploitation look (i.e., **MACHETE & HOBO WITH A SHOTGUN**) of the 70s, the filmmakers behind **FATHER'S DAY** instead embraced the neon nightmare of the MTV culture and the balls-to-the-wall excess of the Reagan Era for a film experience so outrageously violent, sexy and entertaining it must be seen to be believed.

If **POULTRYGEIST: NIGHT OF THE CHICKEN DEAD** and **FATHER'S DAY** have taught me anything it is to never, ever count Troma out. This is a must see/must own film.

FUTURE HUNTERS
Mill Creek / 1986
Reviewed by Brian Harris

Cirio H. Santiago. If the name doesn't ring any bells, this review won't be for you. Those of you "in the know" will agree that the name Cirio H. Santiago could easily have replaced "post-nuke" and seasoned fans wouldn't have batted an eye. Outside of his work for Roger Corman, Santiago's name was synonymous with post-nuke; he was the undisputed heavyweight director/producer of post-nuke cinema, in and outside of the Philippines. As a matter of fact, outside of a few Italian productions, Santiago has made some of my favorite Sci-Fi action flicks.

One such flick is **FUTURE HUNTERS**, an experience so gonzo, so thoroughly stricken with ADHD of the script and direction that nothing less than owning it will suffice.

The year is 2025 and the world has gone to hell after the apocalypse. One group of people determined to set things right seek out the fabled Spear of Longinus (Spear of Destiny), the very weapon that pierced the side of Christ while on the cross. The spear is rumored to be able to give the wielder unlimited power, as well as the ability to travel thru time. A man called Matthew has tracked down the spear and uses it to travel back to 1989 in order to stop the mastermind behind the apocalypse before all is lost. There's only one small problem, he dies no more than fifteen minutes after arriving. Now it's up to amateur anthropologist Michelle and her boyfriend Slade to get the spear to its rightful destination and save mankind!

Wait, a Sci-Fi film about a religious artifact? Oh yeah, shit doesn't just stop there, we also get rookie actor Robert Patrick, bikers, an old school Kung Fu battle between Bruce Le (**THE CLONES OF BRUCE LEE** & **BRUCE AND THE SHAOLIN BRONZEMEN**) and legendary Kung Fu character Silver Fox (played by Jang Lee Hwang), Neo-Nazis, a midget tribe, exploding model helicopters and Amazon women! If that doesn't sound like cult cinema gold to you, nothing will!

The acting was mostly on point though there were a few instances of bad, especially coming from the hulking Bob Schott (**GYMKATA** & **HEAD OF THE FAMILY**). It's forgivable though as Linda Carol had great tits and Robert Patrick's affable, midwestern tough guy role both made for some entertaining cinema. I think the only thing people may really find off-putting is the constant action, yeah that's right I said it, constant, non-stop, never-ending action. Forget catching a breath, the action never let's up for a moment, almost every single scene is packed with running, jumping, flying, driving or fighting. Trust me, look away for a second and you just might find yourself completely lost, that's how fast this film moves.

Believe it or not, this is currently being offered on DVD thru Mill Creek's Sci-Fi Invasion 50 Film box set, so if you're interested be sure to grab that set. Not only can you get this entertaining flick but that particular box set also contains Sergio Martino's **HANDS OF STEEL** and a widescreen print of Ruggero Deodato's **RAIDERS OF ATLANTIS**!

HER PRIVATE HELL

BFI / 1968
Reviewed by Phillip Escott

Norman J. Warren will always be remembered for his classic string of horror movies that reigned throughout Soho's fleapits in the 70s. As well remembered as they are, it comes as a surprise that his earlier output in the ass-end of the 60s isn't as fondly remembered. Especially when the man is also responsible for the UK's first official sex film, **HER PRIVATE HELL**.

The film's condom-thin plot revolves around Marisa, a young Italian woman freshly landed in swinging London and trying to make her way in the British modelling game. However she is soon approached by the sleazeballs of the industry, and they want nothing more than to see her naked in front of the camera.

HER PRIVATE HELL was scandalous upon its initial release in 1967, a time when you weren't allowed to show

Lucia Modunio and her breasts

HER PRIVATE HELL

nipples on screen and any form of coitus was a big no-no. As you can imagine trying to get around that would be nigh-on impossible for a veteran director, let alone a first-timer! Warren handles the material like a gentleman and the film doesn't come across as an exploitation flick in any sense in these pornographic days. Yet he somehow managed to fool the censors into thinking this was a movie of value and that Lucia Modunio's breasts were an integral part of the story – a noble cause, I'm sure we can all agree.

The film wasn't released fully uncut however, some three minutes where still trimmed, which showed ladies getting naked at far-out jazz parties: the material was included in the US release of the film. It's odd to think that a film as classy and restrained as this would have caused a huge fuss when the UK has produced films like **9 SONGS** and **RED ROAD** which are considered high-art and both contain explicit sex. How times change. **HER PRIVATE HELL** is an innocent movie from a decadent era, it remains a fun watch regardless of how tame it appears nowadays and watching Maria trying to avoid the scummiest, nastiest men in Soho is all very amusing.

THE HOUSE BY THE CEMETERY, REVISITED
(Christian Version)

??? / 1981
Reviewed by Joachim Andersson

"The world's first Christian monster/horror film. How does a man of God face a monster? Get this DVD and find out, and you wont believe the surprise ending. This film is not intended for children.

Watch as DR Froydstien comes with a demonic mission to steel peoples cells in an attempt to live forever.

POPE APPROVED!

This film originally directed by Lucio Fulci, is the old 80s Italian shocker made Christian, and re-edited by producer Jeff Teck."

So, some guy on the internet has taken it upon himself to edit his own version of Lucio Fulcis gory classic **THE HOUSE BY THE CEMETERY**, and has been selling it on Amazon. Just from looking at the guy's website, this promised to be something beyond belief. Who the hell would buy such a thing? Well, that would be me. I had to.

It starts with a new title screen - Teckfilms.com and The MentalChurch.com Present a film by Jeff Teck. **HOUSE BY THE CEMETARY REVISITED**, *The Christian Version.* Yes, the asshole actually states that he made the film. While watching this little cheap video animation we are treated to a midiversion of some Psalm or something, still hearing the pianos of the movies original soundtrack until the movie starts with the scene where Bob sees the little girl in the painting of the house. Yes, no sign of the scenes with Daniela Doria and her lover. Was it the boobies perhaps? Boobies are bad and make you go to Hell. Bob tells his mom that the girl told him not to come to the house and when the camera zooms in on the painting we get an animated scene with flames "skillfully" edited into the picture along with a scary cheap synthesizer effect and a text that says:
"Someone may die, pray they don't go to Hell" Oh yes, this is going to be awesome.

The movie then gets going with getting that obnoxious little kid and his parents to the Freudstein house and I'm desperately waiting for more fun stuff. Sure enough, when they arrive at the real estate agency and Bob is talking to the little dead girl, that screen with the flames and the evil sound pops up again, this time with the following little tidbit:

"Hell is not for children, they don't know thier right from left hand" Along with editing, spelling is not Jeff Teck's greatest talent.

They arrive at the house, bicker a bit about Catriona MacColl's nerve pills and all of a sudden (through the magic of bad editing) it is night and the flames pop up again:

"What's next, it's anybodies guess."

Yes, by now I am convinced that God is watching over all of us. Especially when the next scene comes, when Catriona is sleeping and Paolo Malco finds the empty Freudstein folder, with added voiceover from Jeff Teck: "Lord Jesus I come to you because you are good. There's just something about this house, something I don't get. The more I read about you the more I believe. Yet sometimes I feel our lives are in danger. I don't know. I wish I had the answers. The noises, the whining. Something about this house is just different. I hear the sounds that I have to go explore what the sounds are. Oh Lord, help me and my family escape the day of judgment when all will come down upon us. And I know whatever we face down in this house, we can handle it. That's what you are best at, Lord. Bringing things to a good end. I don't know what's through that door, I don't know what's under this house but it could be an evil for this is a sinful planet. Then who could explain it? Lord I just want to thank you in the name of Jesus that you are in control and I just want to thank you for all you do. No matter how spooky this place gets I know I got you! Thank you Lord. Amen."

The original scene is a pretty atmospheric one, showing that old Fulci had some pretty decent movie making skills, greatly helped by Sergio Salvati's excellent photography. This version? Uhm, yeah. When the monologue is finished, Malco hears something behind the cellar door and goes to investigate. Too scary for Jeff Teck, who scissors the proceedings like he is blind, and all of a sudden we cut into a scene next day, in the middle of a sentence. Later on, when Malco is reading his predecessors diary, Teck edits in a short scene where a frantic McColl tries to open the cellar door, and goes back to the diary scene like nothing happened. Why? Only Jeff Teck knows. All of a sudden we come to that classic scene where McColl finds the babysitter wiping the blood off the floor. You know, The "I made coffee" scene. This means that Teck also cut out the scene where the real estate agent meets her maker. This goes for the babysitter scene as well. Surprised? And then we come to the climax that goes all Takashi Miike on us. The movie turns black and white (You know, the tenth generation VHS dub black and white) when Paolo Malco attacks Dr Freudstein, an overdubbed voice says "Lord Jesus help me", the screen is bathed in fog and lightning comes down from above. Then the Earth explodes. The End, the end titles tell us as Catriona MacColl, Paolo Malco and Giovanni Frezza stare.

Okay, this is by far the poorest excuse for a "movie" I have ever seen. The editing is pitiful and seems to be done all random. The last half of the movie is full of skips, graphical errors and loud bursts of static, with the occasional repeating of a scene. Unfortunately the Christian propaganda is kept to the first half so I guess he got tired of it and just went haywire. It has to be seen to be believed.

THE HOUSE BY THE CEMETERY is a fine little gore flick but the script is not exactly logical and rather fragmented, when a Christian hack starts messing about with it, cutting out all the gore, deleting random scenes (the whole thing is just 53 minutes. Go figure) and adding animations that a five year old could have done better it turns into something totally incomprehensible. This is just fucked up. I wish there was a commentary track by Jeff Teck, but I would probably be too afraid to listen to it.

Thank you lord for this little movie and the pleasure it has given me. All the spelling mistakes are taken straight from the movie.

[Editor's Note – How is it this guy hasn't had his ass kicked yet? MADNESS!]

I DRINK YOUR BLOOD

MTI Video / 1970
Reviewed by Mike Haushalter

A band of Satanic hippies roll into a town and begin terrorizing the local folk. They rape a young local girl and her grandpa goes after them. He fails and is dosed with LSD. This bothers his grandson and he gets back at the hippies by feeding them meat pies infected with blood from a rabid dog. They turn into crazed lunatics and begin killing and/or infecting everything in their path. **I DRINK YOUR BLOOD** is a mouth foaming, limb flying, blood splattering, uber drive-in classic. In fact it's a textbook example of great exploitation film making, chock full of sex, violence and mayhem from director David E. Durston. Combining elements of the Manson family, Satanic rites, backwoods vengeance and an actual rabies outbreak Durston fashioned **I DRINK YOUR BLOOD** into an explosive orgy of ultra violence and inhumanity that still packs quite a punch to this day. Durston's wiz bang story is bolstered by some fine performances including Indian actor/dancer Bhaskar's mesmerizing turn as Horace Bones, the film's silk-tongued super evil Charlie Manson stand-in (the kind of crazy cat that would set his sleeping mother on fire just to toast some marshmallows), the beautiful Lynn Lowry as a mute, and Riley Mills as a vindictive grandson. Adding to the infamy of this blood drenched tale of rabies-laced meat pies and Satanic bloodlust is its clever marketing campaign courtesy of producer Jerry Gross

(love the name) who paired **I DRINK YOUR BLOOD** with an old B&W clunker called **VOODOO BLOODLUST** that had been gathering dust on some shelf for a number of years until Jerry picked it up, dusted it off and rechristened it as **I EAT YOUR SKIN**, resulting in one of the most memorable drive-in double features of all time.

For years **I DRINK YOUR BLOOD** had been unavailable on video (other than gray market bootlegs) so MTI's lavish DVD presentation under the banner of its "Fangoria Midnight Classics" label back in 2006 was a welcome addition to many fans collection. It's a beautiful uncut, restored version of the heavily-edited exploitation sickie complete with a host of extras and hidden features including interviews, bios, deleted scenes, audio commentary, a heap of classic drive in trash trailers, Easter eggs.

I EAT YOUR SKIN

VCI Entertainment / 1964
Reviewed by Mike Haushalter

A cancer researcher on a remote Caribbean island discovers that by treating the natives with snake venom he can turn them into bug-eyed zombies. Uninterested in this information, the unfortunate man is forced by his evil employer to create an army of the creatures in order to

LIBIDO MANIA

IL MONSTRO DEL MAR!

Breaking Glass Pictures / 2010
Review by Joachim Andersson

Stuarts Simpson's **IL MONSTRO DEL MAR!** sounds like a wet dream for exploitation hounds on paper. Three slightly unhinged goth chick hitwomen go to a small coastal town somewhere in Australia to relax after a couple of bloody jobs and happen upon Il Monstro Del Mar!, a tentacled sea beast that surfaces from time to time to dine on the locals. Yes, looks good on paper. And it starts so well with an excellent grindhousey scene in black and white where our obscenity spewing heroines dispatch a couple of horny males on a lonely wilderness road before heading into the town. And boredom.

Okay, the biggest problem with **IL MONSTRO DEL MAR!** is that is isn't very entertaining. The story is sound enough but is filled with way too much pointless chatter and wandering around in the picturesque but way too claustrophobically shot town. The characters are interesting but aren't particularly well fleshed out. A couple of flashbacks give us some meat but the movie needed more if we ever were to want any of these mouthy bad ass babes to stay alive. The filmmakers should have worked more on this instead of just wanting them to be straight out of a Tarantino movie. The other characters fare a bit better, especially Kyrie Capri as young girl Hannah who gets involved with the ladies mostly because there is nothing else to do in this run down skeleton of a town other than caring for her grandfather (played by Norman Yemm, an actor decent enough to do something worthwhile out of a character that is there to serve as your average harbinger of doom). There are a few other characters around but they are just monster fodder. Speaking of monster, this is something that the movie does well in a fun and lovingly cheesy way with stop motion and old school effects. There are a couple of good gore scenes and if the movie had had more of those, this movie would have been a winner. Unfortunately, most of this is in the climax. Such a shame.

As it is now, the movie is only 76 minutes including credits and it still feels like it drags. Not a good thing. It is not exactly a bad movie, just a very flawed one.

LIBIDO MANIA

VPS Film-Entertainment / 1979
Reviewed by Phillip Escott

Where do you start with a film like **LIBIDO MANIA**? It's a Mondo movie, only it's not. Think **LET ME DIE A WOMAN** and not **MONDO CANE** and you'll be on the right track. Here Bruno Mattei stages all kinds of kinky antics for the enjoyment of the audience. He may have

conquer the world.

I EAT YOUR SKIN is a rollicking pulp adventure made in 1964 (under the title **VOODOO BLOODBATH**) back in the days when men were men, women were breast-heaving doe-eyed vixens, and every one smoke and drank a lot. I guess Joe Public wasn't ready for this seedy tale of booze guzzling, bed hopping, wife swapping, jet set-ting debutantes, voodoo hijinks, and shambling horrors because it was left on a shelf for seven years collecting dust. The film's fate changed for the better when it was picked up by producer Jerry Gross and given its now infa-mous title **I EAT YOUR SKIN**. It was then paired with **I DRINK YOUR BLOOD** (which had been filmed under the title **PHOBIA**) resulting in one of the greatest double-bills of all time.

Truth be told **I EAT YOUR SKIN** is a real turkey, but I love it, it's like a Thanksgiving feast with all the trim-mings. It's got a bonkers plot, ripe dialogue, cheesy and ineffective monster makeup, and a loopy cast. Somehow all these faults work together to create an exceptional piece of entertainment and fun. For an extra good time pair it up with its cinematic foster sibling **I DRINK YOUR BLOOD** and relive some seventies drive-in mad-ness.

If your looking to add **I EAT YOUR SKIN** to your col-lection go with VCI's release of **THE SWAMP OF THE RAVENS** which is paired up with a decent restored LTB full length print of **I EAT YOUR SKIN** intended this to come across as a serious study in human sexuality, but he's created the complete opposite as the film is hilariously funny for all the wrong reasons.

LIBIDO MANIA 'documents' the findings of Austro-German psychiatrist Richard von Krafft-Ebing's 1886 forensic case study 'Psychopathia Sexualis', which is mostly remembered today for bringing the terms 'sadist' and 'masochist' to a wider audience. It also introduced his findings that homosexuality is, he theorised, was a biological differentiation and not the psychological one that Sigmund Freud would later suggest and not forgetting the then controversial suggestion that martyrdom was an act of hysteria and just a kink for masochists. Ouch.

Being an epic exploitation picture however, Mattei mainly focuses on cramming in examples of paraphilia rather than the actual study and who could blame him? Covering everything from voyeurism to coprophagia, it at least has the scope of Krafft-Ebing's landmark study. Hilarious scenes of a man hanging around ladies toilets' with the hope of catching a lady dropping her bowels so he can go and play with her dookie is then matched by sheer shock value with graphic scenes of a sex change. Variety is indeed the spice of life and that's where **LIBIDO MANIA** earns its stripes and keeps the viewer watching.

Mattei again uses that infamous African stock footage he put in **HELL OF THE LIVING DEAD** to terrible effect, only this time it works. If you watch the Italian cut of the film as opposed to the German cut you'll have a whopping 30 extra minutes of this archive footage that contains an uncomfortable amount of animal cruelty. The German cut focuses more on the sleaze and staged scenarios and works better for it. **LIBIDO MANIA** is an entertaining watch for the sheer 'what-the-fuckery' of it all.

MASSACRE

EC Entertainment / 2001
Reviewed by David Zuzelo

Gorehounds, lend me your ear! **MASSACRE** is one of the films famed for being chopped up and having a bit recomposed into Lucio Fulci's film **CAT IN THE BRAIN**. For years it was the one I was most curious about because it is directed by a true Sleaze Titan, a cinemaniac whose work I really look forward to watching time and time again...Andrea Bianchi! With a laundry list of celluloid sins that includes **ANGEL OF DEATH**, **MALABIMBA**, **STRIP NUDE FOR YOUR KILLER**, **MANIAC KILLER** and one of my favorite Italian zombie films-**BURIAL GROUND**-this guy is Europena Trash Cinema Royalty. I bow down at his name...

I expected a horror film here, given the cool promotional art and the sequence from **CAT IN THE BRAIN**, but

what I got was something entirely different. Horror fans looking for splatter and fleshy penetration get a few glimpses of the red, but this is a sleazy bit of business where horror comes second to all that naughty behavior that comes with the Bianchi pedigree.

MASSACRE opens up with the sequence shown in **CAT IN THE BRAIN** as a prostitute gets chopped up in graphic fashion. A particularly brutal scene, I could not help but notice that the killer is wearing sunglasses and reflects his victim in a shot that looks very close to the American poster for **WATCH ME WHEN I KILL!** All this sequence does is let us know that a killer is on the loose and a young cop is on the case. Luckily, that cop reports to Eurotrash icon PAUL MULLER! I damn near fell out of my chair when he showed up.

The plot proper starts after the slaughter sequence is through however. Horror fans may lean on the fast forward button a bit, but sleaze mavens will be delighted. A bit of violence occurs almost a half hour later-and then it takes to almost the one hour mark for more to arrive. But along the way we get to meet the cast and crew working on a film called **DIRTY BLOOD**, a title I think is damn near perfect for a Bianchi film! The titles roll as our heroine walks through a fog frosted cemetery to the sound of some chanting monks (ahh...Templar Terrors perhaps?)-when she finally joins the circle of hooded figures that are doing the horrific humming things get nasty. Why? I have no clue, but she soon realizes that the skeletal hands

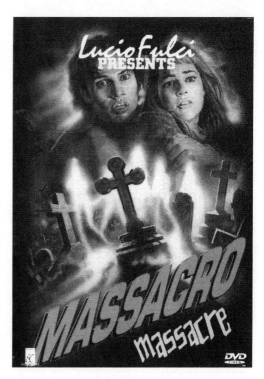

that reach for her are not looking to comfort her heaving breast, or even to cop a feel off the same breast. *THEY COME TO DEVOUR!* Probably THE BREAST as Bianchi has been known to indulge in after **BURIAL GROUND**.

After a minute of running and zombie chest bumping the camera pulls back beyond the crew and the scene is revealed as low budget Italian horror movie. One zombie even bears a nice monster mask resemblance to the magnificent creatures from the **BURIAL GROUND**. What is even funnier is that the actor wearing that ridiculous rubber atrocity pulls it up and declares "This is a shitty film anyways!"

CUT!

With the "horror" out of the way, we get to meet the cast and crew-a bunch of unlikable people that you can only hope Mr. Slaughter in the Shades from the first scene gets hold of quickly. The director of the film is serious about his work though, and he is arranging a séance (oh oh) to get his actors in the right frame of mind. The actors have different ideas as they grope each other's genitals at dinner, plot lesbian seductions and mistreat each other. The lesbian angle is played in true junk cinema fashion-Bianchi jams our face in semi-sensual seduction. Good! This film actually taught me that I love the trash tropes such as this as much as I enjoy massive gore splats in a zombie film. When Liza (Silvia Conti), the perfectly trashy sexpot does a striptease to garner a little Sapphic security, she is interrupted by her loving husband and told to speed up her efforts you know that is classic sleaze. The opening scene is a fairly good Eurogore highlight, but this line is better. "Now you have 24 hours to get that lesbian in bed with us. Otherwise pack your bags and go to the shithouse gutter!" Doubled up with the hot and bothered click track n' Sex Sax music of Luigi Ceccarelli....my brain swells up with joy at the thought of watching it again.

Oh wait, the horror.... so, after the funky séance that is loaded with nearly every off kilter shot Bianchi has used in the past someone starts killing the cast off! Not that we care really, but I could have gone for one more strip tease by Silvia Conti at the least. Most of the violence is off screen barring a few low rent stabbing shots, but I have to tip my hat for excessive post slaughter shots by the ever reliable Guiseppe Ferranti. At the one hour mark the psycho killer from the opening is captured, but looks entirely different... I don't get that part, but it shows that someone else is now the predator. Another Eurotrash connection this film draws for me is that the original killer is captured after attacking a prostitute and her client in the woods. He kills the man quickly of course, but the hooker goes on the run, topless of course. I would swear that this scene is replicated almost exactly in the "Polish" slasher film **FANTOM KILER**.

The finale is exactly what you would expect and delivers, stylishly even, the titular **MASSACRE**. With only Jennifer surviving the night's mayhem she must outrun and outlast the assailant-and when she finally destroys the possessed perpetrator it proves her undoing! Ah well...she was a terrible actress anyways.

MASSACRE is not a good horror film by any standard, but it definitely satisfied my love of Eurotrash and exploitation movies. A few good effects by Ferranti, the awesomely sleazy lesbian seduction story, a hysterically overplayed sequence of a particularly flamboyant actor running through a batch of female impersonations that ends with him strutting around topless as Marlene Dietrich, Maurice Poli staring at a J&B bottle and a tribute to **BURIAL GROUND** make this a great 85 minutes for the right viewer. I may be in the minority, but I liked this film.

With a production company called CINE DUCK how can you go wrong? You can't! This is a good little trashy film made when the Italians had pretty much given up on the genre.

Released by EC ENTERTAINMENT on DVD as part of the Lucio Fulci Presents line in 2001, this is one for the fans of skuzzy late 80s cinema!

MIAMI GOLEM

Action International Pictures / 1985
Reviewed by Brian Harris

TV reporter Craig Milford (David Warbeck) is about to get the story of his life when a lab accident sparks life in a group of cloned cells found within a meteorite, causing the cells to grow at a rapid rate. When those responsible for the project are all murdered and the cells stolen, Milford discovers a link between the cells and an unstable millionaire with grandiose (and under-developed) dreams of ruling the world. With the help of a mysterious woman named Joanna (Laura Trotter) and an alien civilization tasked with protecting the cosmos, he sets out to destroy the now fully formed fetus before it brings the galaxy to its knees.

Alberto De Martino has been doing his thing in cult cinema for quite some time now with some damn good flicks to his credit but none of his films, in my opinion, can so thoroughly boast of being as bad as **MIAMI GOLEM**, and that includes the ungodly bad but infinitely entertaining, **THE PUMAMAN**. IMDb users, trolls and MST2K fans be damned. Seriously though, you'll get thru about 75% of the film before you realize that nothing of any real consequence has happened outside of some hilarious sequences featuring the world's worst hitman. The few short glimpses of the alien "golem" floating in its containment unit were promising, and rather creepy, but one gets the feeling that after it was created by the FX team (lead by Stivaletti!), the rest of the budget was blown on cocaine and airboat rentals. Even an alien visitation, always an opportunity for something cool, was squandered and the alien appeared as Warbeck himself. RIP-OFF!

Normally I could recommend a film based on nudity or gore but Laura Trotter's nudity was far too brief to rub out that easy one, and her face much too ugly to pause on, and there was no damn gore. With such an amazing lineup of writers including Gianfranco Clerici (**DON'T TORTURE A DUCKLING & CANNIBAL HOLOCAUST**), Vincenzo Mannino (**VIOLENT NAPLES & THE NEW YORK RIPPER**) and De Martino himself, one would think we could get something better than a glorified made-for-TV spittoon but clearly that was not to be.

Released by A.I.P. (Action International Pictures) on VHS as **MIAMI HORROR**, this is one Italian production you'll regret scoring on eBay. There's no guilty pleasure factor here, this film is just plain bad.

MURDER OBSESSION
(Follia Omicida)
Raro Video / 1981
Reviewed by Dan Taylor

In recent years I've been pleasantly surprised to discover that despite what my once-cynical self believed, I have

definitely not "seen it all". Not only am I constantly getting turned on to new flicks, genres and stars, but an entire spate of 80s trash cinema that somehow flew under my radar for decades has made its way to my DVD player.

To wit, flicks like **FACELESS** (1987), **DELIRIUM** (1987) and **BLOODY MOON** (1981) have all become favorites that would have blown my mind had I seen them at the time they originally snuck onto these shores. Thanks to Raro Video you can add **MURDER OBSESSION**, Riccardo Freda's mind-boggling genre mash-up to that list.

Unleashed on an unsuspecting public in 1981, **MURDER OBSESSION** (aka Follia Omicida) stars Stefano Patrizi as Michael, a film actor who harbors a dark secret involving the death of his father, a famous maestro frequently referred to as "The Maestro". After finishing his latest film – and nearly killing co-star Beryl (Laura Gemser) while in a homicidal trance – Michael and galpal Deborah (Silvia Dionision) retreat to his family estate for some rest and relaxation. After an uncomfortable night spent with Michael's supposedly-ill mother Glenda (Anita Strindberg) and Oliver The Creepy Butler (John Richardson), they're joined by director and shutterbug Hans (Henri Garcin), his assistant Shirley (Martine Brochard) and Beryl, the near-strangling victim from the opening.

Any expectations that Freda has simply set the stage for a paint-by-numbers Giallo entry are quickly dispatched as the flick zigs and zags between murder mystery, haunted house flick, lingering incest and nightmare fantasy highlighted by Deborah's recounting of an over-the-top bared-titty dream sequence that is easily worth the price of admission. Played excruciatingly straight, **MURDER OBSESSION** will have you watching with slack-jawed amazement right up to its blasphemous ending.

The only other Freda work I'd previously seen was his late 60s thriller **DOUBLE FACE** starring Klaus Kinski and Margaret Lee. I recall being duly unimpressed by that flick when I saw it twenty years ago, but **MURDER OBSESSION** has me itching to break out my copy of **LIZ ET HELEN**, the film's longer and supposedly sexier cut. Sadly, **MURDER OBSESSION** would turn out to be the director's swan song, as it was for the still hot Strindberg who would supposedly settle down with an American millionaire and leave the film world behind.

The Raro Video standard DVD release features a sharp-looking transfer with occasionally muddled audio that one hopes will be corrected for the flick's upcoming Blu-Ray release. Two Italian-language scenes with English subtitles have been inserted back into the flick, though only one really adds anything to the film. Other extras include a full-color booklet and an interview with Sergio Stivaletti who assisted with the flick's oft-crude special effects.

Though the end drags out a bit longer than necessary,

MURDER OBSESSION is a top-notch example of everything that makes off-the-wall Eurotrash – or unique cinema of any heritage – such a worthwhile and rewarding treat. Pair it with John Philip Law's crazoid **BLOOD DELIRIUM** for an 80s double bill that will leave you babbling for days.

THE NECRO FILES
Threat Theatre / 1997

Reviewed by Brian Harris

A crazed serial rapist is on the loose, leaving a trail of half-eaten, mutilated corpses in his wake, and the only people standing between him and and the innocent women he preys on are Seattle police detectives, Sloane and Manners. When they receive a call that he's been spotted in their area, they rush to the scene of a crime and an altercation occurs leaving Manners incoherent and their suspect dead, lying in a pool of his own blood.

Almost a year later, a group of Satanist gather at the rapists grave to conduct a ritual aimed at bringing him back from the dead. Unfortunately for them, he returns with a thirst for bloodshed, flesh and sweet, sweet pussy. Now Sloane and Manners must once again track down the resurrected criminal, now an unstoppable zombie, before he fucks and slaughters his way thru the female population of Seattle. To make matters worse, Manners is losing his grip on reality and the surviving Satanists have called in a demon enforcer, possessing the corpse of a sacrificed newborn, to clean up their magickal mess.

If **THE NECRO FILES** sounds like a low budget gem packed with nudity, gore, hilarious slapstick and atrocious acting, well...that's exactly what it is! Filmmaker Matt Jaissle has crafted one of those rare low budget, shot-on-video horror films that you always hear about but never actually witness for yourself. Saying it's just "good" doesn't do **THE NECRO FILES** justice, it's indie insanity to the Nth degree and from beginning to end, it just gets progressively nuttier. By the time you realize you're watching a zombie fall in love with a blow-up sex doll while being stalked by a flying babydoll, it's far too late, Jaissle and company have got you and the film is almost finished.

As I mentioned above, the acting was TERRIBLE, especially from actor Gary Browning who only appeared to have had one volume setting (LOUD and MONOTONE). Thankfully Steve Sheppard (playing Det. Manners) does his best Dirty Harry impression and ends up saving the day and keeping things interesting. The remaining actors were all hit or miss, as most amateur actors tend to be, but the production didn't suffer from that at all in my opinion.

The three things that really ended up sealing the deal for me was the comedy (written by filmmaker Todd Tjersland), both the dialogue and physical comedy worked

incredibly well. I dare you not to laugh out loud when you see the zombie's 12" junk rise to the occasion thanks to some poorly concealed fishing line. Another positive was the gore, it was out-of-this-world nasty and genuinely gruesome, I was very impressed with the FX work that went into this production. Finally, the nudity. Oh my, yes, the nudity. What can I say? This flick had juggs, big asses, S&M, rape and unshaven, full-frontal, splayed-leg beaver shots; if I didn't know better I could have sworn this flick was made exclusively for me!

I rarely gush so hard (wink wink) over indie horror, especially over the shit being churned out today, so trust me when I say that no horror fan with a sense of humor should be without this film. Add it to your collection!

NU-MERI:
BOOK OF THE NEW SPAWN
(Aihyôka: Nu-meri)
Sxion 23 / 2008
Reviewed by Joachim Andersson

Okay, the first question that popped up in my head after watching this movie was: Who was it made for? Well, me maybe. I do agree to the fact that there can never be enough nasty fish movies and this sucker rates way above your average SyFy movie, both in plot and weirdness. But still, the script needed a bit of tailoring if they really wanted to make a memorable horror movie.

Our heroine likes fish. A lot. No, not in any sexual way (put down your dirty mind, just because this is a Japanese movie.....) but she wants to study them and help protect them. When she isn't carving them up in the fish market of course, where she helped out her family on a regular basis. She also studies marine biology and has gotten an internship at a local fish lab, along with a friend. When they arrive strange things start to happen - her friend tends to wake up staring in the night and after she disappears her body is found in the ocean full of fish bites. Someone is obviously performing unethical experiments on the poor, unsuspecting fish. And then it gets really weird. I don't want to go into any major details to spoil anything, just mention that it involves flying, carnivorous fish heads. Yes. Fish heads.

The only thing is that for a movie that is only 75 minutes long including credits, it is pretty damn slow. Nothing happens until more than half the movie has passed, before that we follow the young girl living her life, meeting friends and praying at any fish related shrine she can find. It's almost like one of the narrator less documentaries following the life of a young Japanese woman. Not that it's totally uninteresting, the actors are decent and it feels fairly unscripted but not very horror movie-ish. When the horrors finally come in the end, they are well staged and really creepy as soon as you accept the flying fish heads which are well made on an obviously low budget. Actually, the general weirdness of the last 15-20 minutes is more than worth the while. The build-up could have been a little bit... different. Still, I like the movie as it is. Recommended if you like your dope a bit odd. Like me.

Another thing. This is a sequel. To a movie that seems to be about bunnies. In a horror movie kinda way. *WTF?*

ON THE PROWL

ON THE PROWL
General Video of America / 1989
Reviewed by Phillip Escott

Jamie Gillis hires a stretched limousine and cruises the streets looking for random guys for Rene Morgan to fuck. All those studs who talk shit about wanting to bang porno-chicks would finally get their chance to prove it, not just to themselves, but to the whole world... Or not, as the case turns out.

ON THE PROWL has been immortalised thanks to P.T. Anderson and his Hollywood epic, **BOOGIE NIGHTS**. What that film did manage to convey through the scene with Roller Girl, is the original film's overall sense of desperation as well as depression. Luckily, or perhaps unfortunately, **ON THE PROWL** doesn't end with a punter getting his face kicked in.

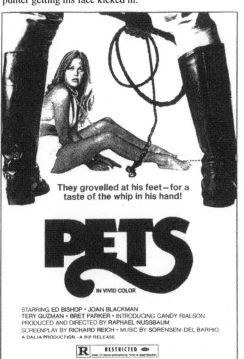

They grovelled at his feet—for a taste of the whip in his hand!

PETS

IN VIVID COLOR

STARRING ED BISHOP • JOAN BLACKMAN
TERY GUZMAN • BRET PARKER • INTRODUCING CANDY RIALSON
PRODUCED AND DIRECTED BY RAPHAEL NUSSBAUM
SCREENPLAY BY RICHARD REICH • MUSIC BY SORENSEN-DEL BARRIO
A DALIA PRODUCTION • A BIP RELEASE

R RESTRICTED

As a porn film it fails, miserably, to achieve the genre's primary objective; to arouse the viewer. Where **ON THE PROWL** does find relevance is in its importance on today's porn market. Jamie Gillis in undeniably the father of Gonzo smut, and this film is the blueprint for which most of today's porn is based upon; no plot, just robotic, uninteresting sex. Even Gillis's best attempts at leading his 'performers' during the scenes ends in failure, as one man has to step down due to being too drunk to maintain his erection.

It's this tragic realism that ultimately makes **ON THE PROWL** watchable, this is car-crash smut that will have you shaking your big head in disbelief. Jamie Gillis would go on to take his Gonzo style of pornography to the extreme with his Human Toilet Bowl series, which could help explain why Gonzo didn't take on for another decade in mainstream porno.

He may be long gone and missed now, but there's no denying the man's legacy and **ON THE PROWL** is only a small part of that; those with an interest in the evolution of American sleaze should seek this out. Otherwise this is strictly for misanthropes who want fuel for their hatred. For a film shot in '89, when AIDS was very much devastating America, it's shocking to see scenes of unprotected sex with complete strangers being portrayed as acceptable.

PETS
Code Red DVD / 1974
Reviewed by Phillip Escott

Candice Rialson, the inspiration for Bridget Fonda's character Melanie Ralston in Quentin Tarantino's **JACKIE BROWN**, stars as Bonnie in the 1974 Grindhouse curio, Pets. Throughout the 70s Rialson played the sumptuous sex kitten in the likes of Drive-in classics **CANDY STRIPE NURSES**, **CHATTERBOX** and **HOLLYWOOD BOULEVARD** until her retirement

in 1979. **PETS** however, would see this sex kitten image pushed to the extreme.

Bonnie is on the run, from what we don't really know, at the start of the film she's being driven, reluctantly, back home by her brother. She's rescued by a bunch of brothers who step in and give her honky brother a beating, she realises that they want a piece of her too and takes off once again. She's soon caught up with a Foxy Brown wannabe, shacked with a man-hating lesbian artist and locked up some chauvinist's cellar-come-zoo! It's hard work being good looking.

PETS is a product of the 70s, there is no other decade where a film of this ilk could have seen the light of day. It's a one-of-a-kind flick that will please fans of Grindhouse cinema with its genre hoping structure and splashing of nudity, thanks to Bonnie's willingness to shed her clothes for anyone at any time! The films unpredictability stems from its refusal to abide by a set of genre rules, and the three tier structure of the films are linked more by theme than content but somehow it all works to the films advantage.

Due to the rarity of the film, all known prints have been pretty banged up and the DVD release as a result is no exception. The grime, crackling and popping of the print all add to the scuzzy nature of the script helping to amplify the Grindhouse experience. Those looking for a piece of Drive-in nostalgia or looking for the best piece of Grindhouse gold need look no further than **PETS**.

PRIMAL RAGE
(Rage, furia primitive)
Code Red DVD / 1988
Reviewed by Phillip Escott

In 1988 Umberto Lenzi renamed himself Harry Kilpatrick, packed his bags and headed off to Florida with Vittorio Rambaldi (Son of Carlo Rambaldi) in tow. Out there they created two of 80s Italian horror cinema's cheesiest entries, Lenzi directed **WELCOME TO SPRING BREAK** while Rambaldi took the helm on **PRIMAL RAGE.**

Baboons are being tested on in a lab; a student breaks in and frees the primate resulting in the student getting bitten and animal being killed when it runs into a police car. Cillian Murphy wakes up in a hospital; he's all alone in the hospital and, more shockingly, the whole of London... Wait, wrong movie! Here the infected student goes about spreading the disease around his campus, to his potential love interests and indirectly three jocks/rapists who all contract the germ and go out on a killing spree during a wild costume party.

PRIMAL RAGE is the superior film of the two made in Florida, but that's hardly a compliment. We have slightly better acting, superior effects work and better pacing but the film is still as inept as **WELCOME TO SPRING BREAK**: Do people really play three-man squash games? In **PRIMAL RAGE** they do! The three men in question though are actually the films chief asset as they truly are 80s villains that you can't help but love for the OTT nature of actor's delivery. No matter how inept the script is, there are always the Rambaldi effects to fall back on, and believe me they help save the day repeatedly during the film.

The effects work here are more akin with Sergio Stivaletti's work on the **DEMON**s films than anything you would normally find in a Lenzi affiliated movie, and the young cast of unknowns - aside from Sarah Buxton, who was also in **WELCOME TO SPRING BREAK** - are backed up by exploitation heavyweight Bo Svenson. The familiarities don't just end there though! Not only did Claudio Simonetti do the music for each film but the 80s epic 'Say the Word' by Kristen also appears here repeatedly during the film for our enjoyment.

TRUE STORY OF A WOMAN IN JAIL: SEX HELL

(Jitsuroku onna kanbetsusho: sei-jigoku)
Synapse Films / 1975
Reviewed by Brian Harris

A group of women sent to a juvenile detention facility for a variety of unsavory crimes await release or sentencing for prison...and...that's about it! Oh yeah, and hot, steamy lesbian sex ensues. While some of you may have read that and thought,"What the fuck? That sounds like shit!" you missed the whole damn point of this amazing film. Did I mention there are a few menstruation gags and some guard-on-inmate rape action? Yeah, all that good stuff too!

Synapse Films is gearing up for an epic gushening of Nikkatsu Roman Porn on DVD, damn near close to 30 releases, including films with titles like **CONFIDENTIAL REPORT: PROSTITUTE TORTURE HELL, NURSES' DORMITORY: ASSY FINGERS"** and **RAPE SHOT: MOMOE'S LIPS!** MY GOD...if that doesn't sound like a Saturday night filled with beer drinking and cock strangling, I don't know what does! The first two films to see release, **DEBAUCHERY** and this one, were a ball to watch for a seasoned sleazemonger such as myself but that might not be the case for many of you looking for generic Skinemax softcore. The title is **SEX HELL** for a reason, if you're not accustomed to WIP films or Roman porn, you probably shouldn't be watching this to start with because it is incredibly offensive and filthy, the film overflows with mutual masturbation, forced sex and violence. It won't be everybody's cup o' pee...er...tea.

The one thing that I loved about **TRUE STORY OF A WOMAN IN JAIL: SEX HELL** was the godawful depressing, nihilistic finale that will take your breath away...that is...if you're not already gasping from severe dehydration and a cramped bicep.

WELCOME TO SPRING BREAK

(Nightmare Beach)
Lionsgate / 1988
Reviewed by Phillip Escott

The 70s belonged to the Giallo genre, but what happens when you're a workman director by the name of Umberto Lenzi and the genre you've been steadily working in is no longer in demand? Why you work in the genre that was directly lifted from it, the Slasher movie! What could possibly go wrong? A lot!

WELCOME TO SPRING BREAK tells the tragic tale of Diablo, a misunderstood gang leader who is incorrectly apprehended for the murder of a local girl. He's sentenced

500.000 STUDENTEN EN ÉÉN NIET TE STOPPEN MOORDENAAR...

19

and delivers a body count. Not to mention it also contains a scene where a biker gang invades a police station to bust out a fellow member; rock and roll!

ZOMBIE 4 AFTER DEATH

(Oltre la Morte)
Shriek Show / 1989
Reviewed by Mike Haushalter

A Voodoo curse on a remote island opens up the gates of hell for the "flesh-eating undead" to appear to devour the living. "With blood spurting, head-bursting, human puppetry, cannibalism, & great zombie gore & FX, who will survive this onslaught of the undead"?

Are you in the mood for some goofy, gooey mindless fun? If so **ZOMBIE 4: AFTER DEATH** from Shriek Show may be just the film for you. The film is an über-gory zombie assault filled with a never-ending supply of bi-polar ninja zombies (sometimes they are slow, sometimes they are super swift.) and a story line thinner than a coked up swimsuit model mainlining Slim Fast. In fact I can sum up the story in 3 words "zombies kill everybody". There is just not any more to it. In a mild twist the zombie hordes seem more intent on doling out pain and infecting the living than using the cast as a snack. Speaking of the cast, other than the appearance of porn star Jeff Striker (billed under his real name Chuck Peyton) as the nominal hero, there's just not much to mention. The whole cast pretty much just runs around looking freaked out waiting to bite it (or be bit as the case may be). Production wise the film looks as if it was shot in a jungle and on some cave sets as quickly and cheaply as possible (which it was).

For those who don't know, **ZOMBIE 4** is not a sequel to **ZOMBIE** or **DAWN OF THE DEAD** or even **RETURN OF THE LIVING DEAD**. It is actuality just a stand-alone feature that someone added the **ZOMBIE 4** moniker to so they could make a quick buck

The DVD release from Shriek Show. Shriek Show's print is a glorious widescreen edition that probably looks better than it did when it was originally released. It also has several nice extras including a heap of previews and interviews with Claudio Fragasso, Candice Daly, and Jeff Stryker.

ZOMBIE 6: MONSTER HUNTER (Absurd)

Ace Video / 1981
Reviewed by Betsy Burger

Let's face it. This movie is of interest to select small groups of people for three main reasons: 1. It is the unofficial

to the death penalty and is electrocuted for a crime he did not commit. Well, that's kinda what the film is about. Naturally a leather clad bike rider comes into town shortly after Diablo's execution and begins to kill the students who have come to enjoy their Spring Break. Who is this person on the bike? Has Diablo come back to avenge himself?

Truthfully, you won't really care as the people in this film are so fucking annoying that you want Diablo to hurry the hell up and waste them at a faster rate. Being a product of the 80s though, the movie is saved by the sheer level of cheese the film has to offer the viewer. Terrible fashion? Check. Terrible hair? Heck yeah. Terribly catchy 80s party anthems? Big check on this one, baby. Lastly, oh so laughable acting? By the bucket load!

WELCOME TO SPRING BREAK is saved by its own uselessness; it's a lot like the runt of the litter in that it came late and doesn't have the same quality DNA shared by its healthier siblings but by golly if that goofiness doesn't make you want to crack a smile and give it a home. The fact that veterans John Saxon and Michael Park's have small roles helps carry the film during its teen comedy-esque opening act before finally finding its Slasher roots sequel to the infamous **ANTROPOPHAGUS.** 2. It, like **ANTROPOPHAGUS**, is among an assortment of movies on videocassette banned in the U.K. in the 1980s, colloquially dubbed "video nasties." 3. It is a must-have for D'Amato completists. (I'm sure there must be hundreds.)

If you have seen, or want to see this movie, you are possibly (what is known by most as) a classic gore hound - you are in it for the cringy violence. **ZOMBIE 6: MONSTER HUNTER** delivers the violence, although said violence often outs itself as embarrassingly fake. (The purpose, after all, is to leave nary a scrap to the imagination.) Young people, new to (ahem) classic film, may scoff at these relatively early attempts to convey impossible feats of cinematic human mutilation. (Yes, dear. That is some rubber-like synthetic compound, yes.) But, I maintain that these "nasty" scenes are worthy of eye-averting, nail-biting, nacho-spewing, drive-in applause. At the very least,I'm fairly confident I can guarantee five or so minutes of nervous laughter throughout.

But maybe there's more to **ZOMBIE 6: MONSTER HUNTER.***

In the late 1970s and the early 1980s, Michael Myers, Jason Voorhees, and Freddy Krueger charmed my generation of Americans. Their movies served to both flout and enforce our parents' simple moral standards. (I say, "simple" because in retrospect, the past is always less complicated. Our tools improve, our knowledge expands, but the present and future – always dicey.) Our parents were born before the sexual revolution. Our parents remembered a time before television.

My own parents lined up to see Universal Studios' **FRANKENSTEIN** in 1931 - which showcased one of the most frightening and sympathetic monsters in history. ... But my generation had Michael, Jason, and Freddy - hideous box office darlings - unstoppable monster-killers who's enduring franchises replaced Universal's monsters in our children's Halloween hearts.

(For ease of use in this review, we're going to pretend that monster movies did not exist before 1978. We will also make believe that art in cinema is so subjective, it isn't even real. Starting now.)

Just as Craven's (brilliant!) Freddy, and (yawn, not worth mentioning) Jason must pay homage to Michael Myers, so too must George Eastman and Joe D'Amato's Mikos Stenopolis. Mikos was crafted more after Carpenter's Michael model than the illustrious Romero zombie empire, as some would have you believe. (I'll concede that brain destruction - the prescribed sure fire-method of death for Mikos - is very zombie-esque, but let's not try to get too geeked out over it.) Aside from some bankable monster schtick, and a decent monster origin story (Mikos' is pretty cloudy) , The real glaring difference between this movie and **HALLOWEEN** and its slasher spawn is a complete lack of naughty teenagers. It is, in fact, completely devoid of sex and sexuality. ... And it's a D'Amato flick!. ...Weird!

The fact that none of the victims has done much of anything wrong, might devalue Mikos somewhat as a sympathetic monster, but not as much as Mikos' back story, which feels like an afterthought. Still, I have pity for this monster; this monster whose face was never reproduced in the form of a plastic mask and marketed to American parents each October. ... Pity - because he is laughed at. Pity - because he is just a guy.

Critics over the years have poked fun at Eastman's non-monster monster, but his character is menacing enough. He's a big fellow after all, and pulls off a crazed look that would send most of us screaming into the street in our skivvies. He is, as the film's Monster Hunter/Priest (Edmund Purdom) explains, quite insane, after all. But he is also quite inventive. He uses the tools at his disposal to create laudable murders, and near murders - the least exciting tool of which, is a pick-ax. (My personal favorite is an oven. Emily (Annie Belle) does an admirable job resisting Mikos' attempts to roast her head. Swell scene.)

As I have have not included a synopsis of the movie in this review, it may be somewhat confusing for all 16 of you who have not yet seen it. Believe me though, there is a story. Here are some things to note while watching: Katya Berger's compass. No justice for hit and run drivers. Ominous rummy. Ram's QB Josh MacDougal (whodat?) ...And if anyone can tell me what that is on TV that so upsets Kasimir Berger, I would appreciate it.

*Nope. Honestly, I can't imagine Eastman snatching the final page from his Smith-Corona (a la Steven J. Cannell) and proudly proclaiming, "FIN! - A MASTERPIECE!" ... No one ever said it was about anything but the cash.

EMANUELLE

The Classic Exploitation Series Encapsulated

by Mike Haushalter

EMANUELLE IN BANGKOK
(Emanuelle Nera: Orient Reportage)
Severin Films / 1976

Emanuelle prowls the steamy underbelly of Bangkok in what amounts to a passionless softcore travelogue. This Joe D'Amato helmed effort is one of Laura Gemser's least inspired outings (not as bad as her performance in **EROTIC NIGHTS OF THE LIVING DEAD** mind you) and even in the love scenes she shares with her then husband Gabriele Tinti she seems like a cold automaton devoid of emotion and lust. In its favor the film has plenty of other sexy women displaying their goods and it offers up a beautiful look at the people and places of Bangkok and is chock full of local filler... I mean color.

BLACK EMMANUELLE, WHITE EMMANUELLE
(Velluto Nero)
Severin Films / 1976

Meadow muffins, dung, shit, poop, manure, excrement, feces whatever you call it crap is crap. Take for instance **BLACK EMMANUELLE, WHITE EMMANUELLE** an Emmanuelle film in name only (fan favorite Laura Gemser isn't even named Emmanuelle in the film she's a model named Laura) that has also gone under the names **BLACK VELVET, NAKED PARADISE, EMANUELLE IN EGYPT** and **SMOOTH VELVET, RAW SILK** but like I said no matter what you call it, it's still crap.

I am sure the producers of this film would have liked us to believe that the grim, slow moving misogynistic plot they were trying to force feed us had some sort of deep meaning beyond its sandy vistas and glimpses of flesh. An allegory perhaps about the plight of starving third world nations or a denouncement of the genocides taking place in same said nations. Who knows maybe they did but they failed, and the zombie like performances from Laura Gemser and Al Cliver don't help and neither does the bland look at me antics of Annie Belle. About the only plus is lots of bare skin but since bare skin is only a Google click away that's not saying much.

BLACK EMANUELLE 2
(Emanuelle Nera No. 2)
Severin Films / 1976

Buxom Sharon Lesley (Shulamith Lasri) makes her first and only screen appearance as lovely nympho black Emanuelle in the simply titled **BLACK EMANUELLE 2** (her only appearance in anything it seems a shame really she is quite shapely).

In this sequel Emanuelle is a amnesiac supermodel trying to regain her memory with the help of a very hands on psychiatrist who tries to sift through her Freudian nightmares of incest, nymphomania and lesbian longings.. It's sort of a mildly diverting erotic take on Akira

Kurosawa's **RASHÔMON**. Over all it isn't much to shout about. it's a bit slow and dull and not very fresh either. It does however feature decent eye candy, particularly the previously mentioned voluptuous charms of Sharon Lesley.

EMANUELLE IN AMERICA
Blue Underground / 1977

Includes the horse masturbation scene! Really what more do you need to know than that? What's that the horse masturbation scene isn't enough info? You want to know more? Really? This is like my 6th Emanuelle film in a row and you still want to know what it's about?

Well **EMANUELLE IN AMERICA** stars Laura Gemser and was directed by Joe D'Amato (does anybody else think that Robert De Niro would be perfect casting if they make a film about Joe?). Storywise it's an overlong episodic gathering of sexy vignettes chock full of nudity and softcore sex (and occasional hardcore inserts) that will probably only be of interest to fans of old school smut. Oh and of course some infamously staged faux snuff footage that is pretty shocking even in today's world of hardcore violence. Did I mention the horse masturbation scene? There was a sticker on the box of the first copy that I bought of the film that actually said "includes the horse masturbation scene"

EMANUELLE AROUND THE WORLD
(Emanuelle - Perché violenza alle donne?)
Severin Films / 1977

Emanuelle (Laura Gemser) travels across the globe on a journalistic crusade to put a stop to violence against women (giving the films producers ample opportunity to exploit violence against women). This is very gritty and grim viewing with more violent rapes on display then many women in prison efforts of the time (in fact it's as mean-spirited and sordid as one of the many Nazi prison camp films of that era). Some of the other lurid charms of the film include a touch of bestiality (canine and snakes), some lesbian lust and several orgies.

This time out Laura gives a warm and charismatic performance that lives up to her legendary status as a cult star reminding the viewer just why she is famous. Eye candy is also supplied by blond beauty Karin Schubert (**BLACK EMANUELLE**) who shares a very sexual oil rub down with Gemser and is the victim of the films most vicious rape. Severin's single-disc European edition of the film offers up an additional 4 minutes of hardcore footage but otherwise appears to be the same print.

SISTER EMANUELLE
(Suor Emanuelle)
Severin Films / 1977

Emanuelle (Laura Gemser) renounces her life of lust to become a Nun. When faced with a whirlwind of temptation brought on by a teenage nymphomaniac (Mónica Zanchi) and a horny escaped criminal, will she be able to stay true

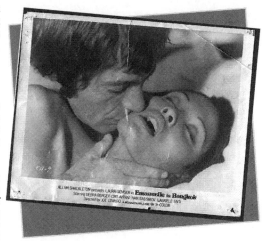

to the ways of the cloth?

SISTER EMANUELLE is a simmering pot boiler of lust, lies, and sacrilege; a steamy mix of naughty school girls and Nunsploitation that will please almost any softcore smut fan. I am not sure if it was the challenge of sharing so much screen time with super sexy Mónica Zanchi (zealously portraying a nymphomaniac vixen) or a change in her meds but Laura Gemser truly shines in this outing, giving a sizzling hot performance worthy of her infamy. The film also stars Gabriele Tinti, Dirce Funari (**EROTIC NIGHTS OF THE LIVING DEAD & PORNO HOLOCAUST**), and Rick Battaglia. This was my favorite of the many recent Emanuelle releases as it contains a number of very hot lesbian trysts and lacks the nasty edge many of the others have. In fact it has a light touch of humor throughout that the other films could have used as well.

EMANUELLE AND THE WHITE SLAVE TRADE
(La Via Della Prostituzione)
Severin Films / 1978

EMANUELLE AND THE WHITE SLAVE TRADE is a potpourri of seventies free love, sex slaves and lavish travelogue footage; a jaunty romp full of sleaze and tease that is sure to please Laura Gemser fans. This rare Euro flesh fest would mark the end of Joe D'Amato and Laura Gemser's official Black Emanuelle collaborations and, to his credit, Joe garners a fabulous performance out of Ms. Gemser in this outing showing her off at the top of her game, full of life, charm and sensuality. While not quite the deliciously dirty farewell to the series the box promises, it's still loaded with a dozen or more lavish nudes, several sexy couplings and a climatic bowling alley punch up between a gang of thugs and a heroic tranny with mad Kung Fu skills. That's well worth the price of admission.

James Bickert (**DEAR GOD NO!**) Talks Bikesploitation
Interview conducted by Brian Harris

*While so many others out there aspire to re-create "grindhouse" cinema, one man is continuing the tradition of true drive-in exploitation with only one damn thing on his mind...blood, boobs and badass bikers. Okay yeah that's three things, fuck you, get back to your bitch seat and shut up! Exploitation fans, grab you some brew and a broad and check out this wild interview with James Bickert, director of **DEAR GOD NO!** and head honcho over at BIG WORLD PICTURES.*

Thanks for taking the time out to do this interview for the zine, James. Let's talk about DEAR GOD NO!, why go with a Bikesploitation film when everybody out there seems to want to do just straight up horror? It probably would have been easier, right?

Yeah, it sure would have been easier to do a found footage ghost story, zombie flick, pussy vampire film or torture porn masquerading as art. It's not what I tend to watch so we decided to make something the total opposite of the productions you see today. I knew it would be financially risky but the most important thing was to create a lost VHS discount bin regional drive-in film from the 70s. The crap I watch and study with a passion. A flick completely stripped down from the stylized directors, actors and technology of today. I've never felt the faux grindhouse movement has accurately captured the little quirks of the exploitation films I love so that was the goal. I find seeing the strings so to speak refreshing. I didn't want the flaws to be in-jokes but part of a intertwined aesthetic charm and nostalgia. Distribution be damned. **DEAR GOD NO!** was complete artistic freedom for better or worse. We give

the viewer enough time to masturbate between our hidden themes. I've seen every biker film so it seemed natural to make a new one that me and my buddies could drink beer with for years to come. I think we did a good job of not making a mockery of exploitation cinema and treating the genre with respect.

That's a great point you brought up about in-jokes and the mockery of exploitation. Do you feel the whole faux-sploitation movement has hurt or helped exploitation? It seems films like GRINDHOUSE, MACHETE, HOBO WITH A SHOTGUN, RUN, BITCH RUN and NUDE NUNS WITH BIG GUNS have done quite a bit to introduce exploitation to the mainstream (and younger) viewers but has it been in a respectful way, in your opinion?

It's helped and hopefully will encourage people to seek out older films. Nobody has gone total **LOST SKELETON OF CADAVRA** with it yet. **ISLE OF THE DAMNED** did to some degree but it's heart was in the right place. You're going to run across the occasional fanboy that will insult everything because they think **MACHETE** is the ultimate form of exploitation but anyone reading Wildside Cinema knows better. Most of these films are homage to TROMA & CANNON. Which is great, but there is a much richer history to the genre. Hell, dating all the way back to the 20s. With **DEAR GOD NO!**, I was going for a CROWN INTERNATIONAL vibe. For the most part I've liked all the modern exploitation films but my emphasis is more on the 60s and 70s. Maybe more drive-in than 42nd street. Out of all of them I felt **RUN BITCH RUN** was the most authentic and I look forward to seeing **NUDE NUNS WITH BIG GUNS**. Astron 6's **FATHER'S DAY** mocks the genre but it's a total hoot. A really great film. My emphasis is on creating a specific type of experience that conjures up the forbidden trashy trailers of my youth. Even faux grindhouse at it's worst is better than *PARANORMAL ACTIVITY 12.*

Oh man, Crown International had some bad ass films under their belt! I mean HELL ON WHEELS, HELLCATS, WILD RIDERS even PINK ANGELS, that kind of stuff is definitely more drive-in culture than grindhouse culture. Do you think some folks missed that when watching you film? I'm sure there are some critics/websites that didn't "get" DGN.

Nah man, it's been very well received within the genre. Outside our niche it's hated but we didn't make it to go mainstream. The blogs have been fantastic and great supporters. It's just amazing at how many well educated cinema junkies there are on the internet. They seem to get it right off the bat and appreciate the use of film, WTF! moments, subversive technique and attention to detail. We did have a water marked rough cut stolen from our sales agent at IFM in Berlin that is being bootlegged apparently in Europe. We tried to reason with one guy so he might hold off until the DVD release. He saw it as a personal attack and started claiming the schtick that art is free and we are an evil corporation. Far from the damn truth. We all work shit jobs and just want to keep making the movies we love. Anyway, he has launched an attack on our IMDB page driving our rating down to nothing in a matter of a week, slamming us on message boards and posting bad reviews. We did a bunch of DIY theatrical runs, festivals and conventions so it was irritating to see 18 months of hard work destroyed by a delusional pirate. But fuck it, what are you going to do and who cares anyway. It was good to take a lashing and keep grounded in reality. It's just the world now. I'm not interested in breaking into the commercial film business and selling myself at cocktail parties. I'm going to make what I want to watch. He's probably named Todd so he is extra pissed. I would be too.

I hear from a few filmmakers that the online bootlegging and shit is definitely an inconvenience but really only affects bad films and most of the people who download it illegally are likely the ones that would never have purchased it anyhow. Do you feel that's correct?

I agree. It's just annoying. These idiots will download a model train video and bitch that it's full of model trains and didn't have Wolverine. I think they compare everything to the **X-MEN** movies. (laughing) It blows my mind. I can't watch films on a computer or phone. I like it big and outdoors.

You've got a genuine passion for Exploitation Cinema, do you dig biker films specifically or all kinds of exploitation?

All of it. From every corner of the planet. I much rather watch 70s porn actors fist fighting in **HONKY TONK NIGHTS** or a big green dude with snakes coming out of his back ripping women's tops off in **ZUMA** than some CGI spectacle. I love all old cinema from Biker, Roughies, Eurospy, Giallo, Hicksploitation, JD Films, Indonesian Flying Head Movies to even Bunuel, Fellini, Goddard, Kurosawa and Bergman. Hell, anything produced by New World Pictures is a religious experience. Lately I've been watching women in prison films from the 30s. The WIP genre is the one I usually fall back on. Something in the exploitation genre will usually get me stuck into consuming a sub-genre or body of work from an actor or director. I once attempted to watch every Vic Diaz film and ended up with the guy tattooed on me. I doubt there is anyone in the Philippines with a **BIG BIRD CAGE** / Diaz tat. Here is this idiot walking around Atlanta with one. The sheer amount of directors and genres... I built a drive-in in my backyard! That's how deep my sickness goes. I grew up around drive-ins so mosquito repellent and popcorn oil

must be in my blood and slowly rotting my brain.

That sounds just like me, right on down to Diaz worship and loving gonzo flicks like ZUMA. Some of my favorites are the ones that blow my mind with wild shit like THE SEVENTH CURSE, BARE BEHIND BARS, MYSTICS IN BALI and NORTHVILLE CEMETERY MASSACRE. Which exploitation/trash films have you seen that could eternally entertain you with untold amounts of sleaze and "WHAT THE FUCK?" moments?

Don't get me started on **BARE BEHIND BARS**! That's a masterpiece. All the films you mentioned are gold. **NORTHVILLE CEMETERY MASSACRE** definitely had some influence over our art direction. The WTF? moment is essential and can burn an image into your brain eternally. I really like the professor who hypnotizes girls so he can put snakes on them in **DELINQUENT SCHOOL GIRLS**. They also throw in some unrelated naked breasts on a trampoline which was a joy. The LSD house cats in **SWEET SUGAR** was wonderful and who can ever forget the Chinese Popeye in **THE DRAGON LIVES AGAIN**! I watch a ton of Godfrey Ho films because you just can't get that many WTF? moments per frame. Asians in blackface, exploding crabs, ninja torpedoes, etc. It's nonstop. The self imposed profanity censorship in **HARD TIMES FOR ARCHIE** is hilarious, the Nixon mask dude's ever changing t-shirts in **THREE WAY WEEKEND**, the post apocalyptic rejects walking around a beach resort in **W IS WAR**, the women that look like Dee Snider in **INTREPIDOS PUNKS**... all of **CROCODILE EVIL** and **RAW FORCE**. My favorite is the bus ride jump cut sex scene in Paul Glickler's **THE CHEERLEADERS**.

Being the devoted trash cinema fan you are, what are some of your most prized pieces in your film collection?

Sonny Chiba in **WOLF GUY** is pretty damn entertaining. You know I've always been a big fan of Vincent Price in **CONFESSIONS OF AN OPIUM EATER**. That's a trashy gem that really delivers and I'm surprised it isn't more popular. **SUDDEN DEATH** with Robert Conrad vs Don Stroud in the Phillipines. That one has Sid Haig & Vic Diaz. **WOMAN HUNT, DEATH WEEKEND, THE OUTFIT, DEVIL WOMAN, WOLF DEVIL WOMAN, TRUCK STOP WOMEN, GAME SHOW MODELS, BLACK OAK CONSPIRACY, BRUTE CORPS, OPEN SEASON, CAGED BEAUTIES, DEADLY SILVER ANGELS, KILLERS ON WHEELS, NIGHT OF THE COBRA WOMAN, MAG WHEELS, THE BANG BANG GANG, HOT CIRCUIT, THE CARHOPS, CHERRY HILL HIGH**... Jeez. I could go on forever. I'm searching for an uncut copy of Barbara Peter's **STARHOPS**. Maybe I'll get lucky with a Greek VHS one day.

VHS is really making a comeback in film geek circles, it's become the new vinyl, so to speak. DGN! is one of those films that almost demands to be released as a VHS, cardboard sleeve, big box and all. Have you considered releasing a limited amount for the hell of it?

Actually we have released very limited editions on VHS in a clamshell at Pollygrind, Corpsedance, Zinema Zombiefest, Arizona Underground Film Festival and The South Alabama Film Festival. Each one was signed and numbered with a different cover. I just finished a run of 25 that I'm taking to Cinema Wasteland tomorrow.

Speaking of all that cinematic gold, the artwork you got from Tom Hodge of The Dude Design was fucking amazing, it represented your film perfectly. Exploitation cinema used to really depend on gorgeous artwork and salacious taglines to draw folks in and your title and poster really nailed that. How did you and Tom decide on this particular design for DEAR GOD NO! and what were you looking for?

It was all Tom. I just told him I wanted naked women. I've been an exploitation poster collector and graphic designer for many years. I designed several promotional posters but nothing was really grabbing me. Being so heavily involved in every aspect of the film, I needed some new eyes and a fresh angle. Tom was the right man for the job. I know how irritating clients can be so I sent him about 100 stills and let the guy do his thing. His large scale spin was what it needed. He's currently working on the poster for **FRANKENSTEIN CREATED BIKERS** so we can get some Cannes pre-sales. I took some stills of a lovely topless lady licking some dynamite and he is off and running. My only input for this one was naked women and cop cars blowing up! He's rockin' the biker / mad doctor look and created a wonderful logo. The guy is

5 QUESTIONS FOR JETT BRYANT

Jett, how did you meet James and end up being cast for the role of, well, Jett in DEAR GOD NO!?

I used to be his boss at the Dong N' Bong. I don't know, I'm just that awesome I guess. Jimmy calls me and says "I'm making the best biker movie ever, you in?"

Are you looking forward to returning to the role in the DGN! sequel FRANKENSTEIN CREATED BIKERS and the DGN! prequel, HELLRAISERS 69?

Absolutely not. My mother hates me. Role? I am Jett. This isn't a character it's a way of life. It's how I live. So you ask if I'm looking forward to it....I'll fuck it in the ass... bring it on!!! If you thought we were fucked up in the first one you haven't seen anything yet I'll rape your brain and call it hamburger helper, it's all the same to me.

When you're not playing a bad-ass biker, you're a bad-ass tattoo artist in real life. How did you get your start in the tattoo industry and where are you currently slinging fine ink?

After struggling getting attention in the artistic community I submitted my profile to the Artist Institute of Atlanta those queens rejected me for drawing Tippy the Turtle taking a dump on a one-eyed pirate. I don't scrape that dog shit off my boot, I just let it dry.

Broads and beer or warm cocoa and a ski lodge?

Scolding hot cocoa on the bitch as I crack open a PBR and burn down the ski lodge with her inside.

What three things could you tell readers about Jett (the DGN! biker) that they didn't get from the movie?

1. I don't eat puppies, only pussy.

2. I'm only half as rapey as I was in the movie but I drink twice as much.

3. Unlike most of my friends, I don't have herpes.

BIG WORLD PICTURES PRESENTS

DEAR GOD NO!

a bad-ass and we connected right away over 70s cinema, posters and ballyhoo. His art has been a major part of our success.

Now there's a flick I'm dying to hear more about! Your second feature FRANKENSTEIN CREATED BIKERS, what's it about and what are the influences going into that film? Will Jett be returning for another lead role in that?

Jett is back. You can't stop him. While **DGN!** had the look and tone of Crown International, I want this next project to take on some elements of a Carlos Aured or DeOssorio film so a tighter film grain and dolly work is going to be necessary. It will be much bigger in scope. The themes in **DEAR GOD NO!** were about parenting, parental fears and selfishness. **FCB** explores confinement, addiction and being emotionally trapped. It's like a Paul Naschy werewolf flick turned into a biker film crossed with **THE BRAIN THAT WOULDN'T DIE** and Filipino action. If that makes any sense. Our big hope is to do **HELLRAISERS 69** the **DGN!** prequel a month later and put together a traveling Drive-in roadshow with bands for summer 2013. That's a long way off and a million headaches to come but that's the goal. **HELLRAISERS 69** will be straight up New World Pictures mixed with 60s Russ Meyer and lead to the events at the beginning of **DEAR GOD NO!** There is some **SAVAGE SEVEN & RACE WITH THE DEVIL** in that script too.

Shit, a new film and a prequel to DGN!, you're going to be busy as hell! Let's talk about the business angle for a

minute, you've been doing festivals (and doing well) and the websites are showing you love, how is distribution looking right now? Are there offers on the table?

We had quite a few distribution offers but they were very similar to the one I inked back in 1999 with a popular distributor. It didn't turn out well. They sat on the film for 3 years, poorly replicated it and didn't accurately report sales. I know some people that after the distributors expenses haven't made a dime from even major labels. There really isn't any good information out there on who is honest so we decided to make our domestic label. That way we could remove the distributors 50% and avoid the sketchy accounting. Our label Big World Pictures is launching a loaded **DGN!** DVD-9 on June 5th along with streaming and a limited edition signed 1440 x 1080p HD Blu-ray. The best part is we get to determine our own ad campaign. We're running full page ads in Rue Morgue & Fangoria in June and Horror Hound & Easyrider a few months later. Archstone / Tombstone is our international sales agent and they are taking the film to Cannes in May. I wouldn't have the patience for international sales. The tax forms alone were wrist-cutting.

James, I really appreciate this interview man, you're a trash fan after my own heart and a stand-up filmmaker with some great ideas. When FRANKENSTEIN CREATES BIKERS and HELLRAISERS 69 is ready would you be willing to sit down and talk with me again?

Oh, hell yeah. We need to grab a beer and talk about genre film. I'll let you ramble on next time. Cheers!

CHANG 張徹 CHEH

An Auteur of Violence and Brotherhood
By Bennie Woodell

Chang Cheh's film style is one of the most recognizable and influential styles in Hong Kong cinema. Chang, one of the Shaw Brothers' most prolific filmmakers, directed more than eighty films. He influenced an entire generation of filmmakers, most notably John Woo who was his protégé and assistant director during the early seventies. He took a genre of film that was violent, and made it more violent, bloodier, and beautiful to watch.

Generally, the martial arts films were very formulaic. The storyline didn't really matter because the hero was usually trying to avenge somebody's death, or got into trouble and had to fight for his life. The story and characters never mattered; it was the fights that were the most important part of the film.

Chang Cheh changed the genre of martial arts movies because he started to make the script just as important as the action. In fact, the action didn't drive the script, the script drove the action. There was a reason for every fight that broke out. His actors developed the characters into human beings, instead of them being just brainless fighting machines. Ti Lung did such a great performance in **BLOOD BROTHERS** that he won the Golden Horse award for best actor. The characters would teach lessons to the audience on heroism, chivalry, and the importance of friendship, or brotherhood.

Chang's films and fights overflow with the theme human mortality. One of the most important aspects of Chang's films is that no man, good or bad, is invincible. We're never quite sure while we're watching one of his films which characters will live to the end. A hero who seems to be the most powerful and skilled fighter can very well end slain by the enemy, or sometimes his friend. Chang is trying to break down the belief that the hero(s) will come out on top no matter what, and this is a reoccurring theme throughout his films.

From the very beginning of **BLOOD BROTHERS**, we know that Chang Wen Hsiang, David Chiang, is on trial for the murder of Ma Hsin I, Ti Lung. The information that is not given to us is that Ma killed Huang Chung, Chen Kuan Tai, so he could be with his wife. In a way that murder could be foreseen because of the affair between Ma and Mi Lan, and we know Ma will let nothing stand in his way of getting what he wants. What comes as a surprise, though, is that Chang is sentenced to death at the end. He is the true hero; he took revenge for his brother, and defeated the evil in society, but he was still killed. Even though he killed an unjust and corrupt official, and fully admitted to it without them needing to use torture, he still killed an official and no leeway was given.

Quite possibly the biggest death count of heroes comes from the film **THE HEROIC ONES**. The film starts out with thirteen generals/brothers. By the end only five of them are left alive, none of which are main heroes, but background characters. Brothers Four and **Twelve** were cause of death of the other six through deceit. Although justice does prevail and the evil brothers are slain, the film is a testament that even the noblest and chivalrous heroes are susceptible to death.

THE FIVE DEADLY VENOMS has a different way of dealing with the death of heroes. The only hero that dies is Li Ho (Lo Meng) the toad character. He is supposed to be the character that cannot be killed because his skin cannot be penetrated and harmed. The villains build an Iron Maiden to attack his weak spot and make him completely vulnerable. After they uncover the spot, Li Ho isn't the super human he was before; instead he is very much a mortal and is easily defeated. He can no longer defend himself and the villains easily dispose of him after this by suffocating him at night. Chang is once again showing us that no man is invincible, that everyone has a weakness that can bring about his downfall and death.

Another theme that is very prevalent in Chang's films is the theme of deception, people not being what they seem to be. The characters think they can trust someone because they are their brother, whether it's in the literal sense or metaphorical. There is always somebody who takes that strong trust and uses it for their own gain. I don't think Cheh is saying not to fully trust your closest friends, or brothers, but instead he's giving somewhat of a warning to never let your guard fully down.

The film **BLOOD BROTHERS**, takes the deception by a brother to the metaphorical sense of the word. Huang Chung and Chang Wen Hsiang try to rob Ma Hsin. The three end up joining together and become "God-Brothers". One day Ma Hsin falls in love with Huang's wife, Mi Lan. They avoid each other when the others are around but secretly long for each other. Ma Hsin decides to take the Confucian exams so he will be able to become a government official so they would have a great life. The two don't hear from him for awhile, but then get the message to come and join his army.

When Ma Hsin sees Mi Lan again, they start up where they left off. Ma Hsin decides that he wants her for himself. He gets Huang to go on a mission with his Royal Guard, but the plan is when they get out far enough to

just kill him. Chang knew about the affair, and when he heard about the mission he went after Huang. Of course Huang wouldn't believe that Ma Hsin was having an affair with his wife and that he wanted him dead. He refused to believe the mission was a lie to deceive and kill him. He accused Chang of being jealous of him and attacked him. Further down the road the guards attacked Huang and killed him.

Chung thought the wrong person was deceiving him. He chose his leader who was also his brother, over his closest companion. He trusted Ma Hsin wholeheartedly and wouldn't believe he would do anything to hurt him. Ma Hsin used his authoritative power to deceive Chung. Either way he'd have to go on the mission because if he didn't go, it would result in his beheading. This form of deception could be Cheh's way of saying not to entirely trust authority, in this case the government. A person in power will do what he has to in order to stay in that position or get a higher position.

In the film **THE HEROIC ONES**, deception by a brother is taken to the extreme literal sense. There are thirteen brothers who are generals under their fathers. Brothers Four and Twelve despise Brother Thirteen because he gets all the glory from their father. Brother Thirteen, Xiao, does not realize the sibling rivalry; in fact he even saved the two from being executed by their fathers' command. The

THE HEROIC ONES

father listened to Chun and sent the two brothers to run a military camp. It is quite obvious that he never read The Art of War because Sun Tzu says "If troops are loyal, but punishments are not enforced, you cannot employ them" (123). He was supposed to punish the two for going against orders but backed down, therefore he should not have sent them to run another camp, and ultimately that would have saved Chun's life.

The two brothers made up a very deceptive plan to get rid of Xiao. While their father was passed out from drinking too much, Brother Twelve snuck in and stole his sword from him. They took the sword to Xiao and told him that his father wanted to see him because he was angry that Xiao left the compound when he saw the city of Bianlong was on fire. Of course Xiao believed his brother, not just because he had the sword but because they were brothers. They took him to a tent, and told him they had to tie him up to show good faith to his father, Xiao went along with it. They started to tie his limbs to horses outside of the tent, and when he tried to get up they said he was showing disrespect to their father if he didn't do this act. After everything was set, they told Xiao of their deception, ran out and the horses ran tearing Xiao's limbs apart. This could have been avoided if Xiao would have not put so much trust in his brothers.

All the brothers trusted each other very well, even to the very end. When the remaining nine brothers circled Four

and Twelve for surrender, they walked up to them to grab their swords without worry. When they got close enough, Four and Twelve stabbed the two that came forward. The two deceived the others in this manner one more time before it was realized they weren't going to surrender, and they were killed.

In the film **THE FIVE DEADLY VENOMS**, to enhance the idea of people not being what they seem to be is shown through an interesting way. There were five students who didn't know each other because they didn't all train together, they didn't use their real names, and they wore masks to cover their identity. Through a murder by the Centipede and Snake, the other students come out. One by one they find out who each other is, and go against each other for their master's treasure.

There are two big deceptions in the film. The first one involves Li Ho, or the Toad. He is framed for the murder of his Master's friend who held the secret for the treasure. His good friend Ho Yung Sin was a General, but he was on a mission. Ho knew Sin was good friends with Ma Chow. When Chow brought Ho a meal, he didn't trust him at first; he waited til Chow tasted it in front of him. After he saw it was safe he started eating.

Hung Wen Tung, who was the Snake, wanted to find Ho's weak point to break his skin armor. He drugged some food and had one of Chow's guards bring it to him saying it was from Chow. This time Ho didn't wait for it to be tested because the last time the food was safe, and he now trusted Chow. That was his fatal mistake because the drugs kicked in and he passed out.

The other deception took place at the final battle. Ho Yung Sin, the Lizard, and Yang Tieh set off to fight the Snake and Centipede. They met up with Chow who left the government, and he went along to fight. He waited in the background most of the fight, then came out as the Scorpion. He was "friends" with both sides but merely used them as a tool to get everyone together so he could kill them all and have the treasure to himself.

The idea of the characters not knowing one another's identity was a good way to get the idea across that no one is what they seem. At first the characters were reluctant to trust one another, but when they started to it was their inevitable downfall. I think Cheh is trying to say in this film that everybody wears a mask, and sometimes you won't really know who a person is until it's too late.

The theme of brotherhood is something that is prevalent in all of Chang's films. Brotherhood could be taken in two ways; one is that the characters are actual brothers, or in the case of most of his films they are sworn brothers who would risk their lives for each other. A brother is a companion who can be entrusted with your own life. Brothers will do anything for each other without fearing anything, even death.

In **BLOOD BROTHERS** Huang and Chang are brothers in the sworn sense. They rob Ma Hsin and get away. He follows them and ends up joining their brotherhood. They fight against a rebel army together and win to take over the base and troops. Huang and Chang are very supportive of Ma Hsin's goal of taking the Confucian exams and becoming a part of the government. While he's away making a name for himself, they remain at the base very loyal to him waiting for when he sends word that they should come join up with him. After Huang's death Chang seeks vengeance and goes to fight Ma Hsin knowing that either way he will not come out of the fight alive. He might die at the hands of Ma Hsin, or if he kills Ma Hsin he knows that the troops would not let him leave. He is fine with this because without his brother he has no one, and would rather right the wrong and join up with Huang soon. He defeats Ma Hsin, and confesses to the court that he killed him. In turn they kill him, but it does not matter to him, he did what was right for his brother.

In **THE HEROIC ONES** the thirteen brothers are actually related. They are all bonded together by actual blood and work under their father. Since they are actual brothers, it's understandable why Xiao pleads to his father to save the lives of Brothers Four and Twelve; and also why at the end the brothers that are left keep giving Four and Twelve chances to surrender instead of killing them.

In **THE FIVE DEADLY VENOMS**, we get to see brotherhood from both the heroes side and the villains side. In the beginning the Master tells his student Yang Tieh that in order to defeat the ones causing trouble, he has to team up with one of the others. The student is forced to find one of them and form a brotherhood, which in the end he teams up with Ho Yung Sun. Together they figure out how they can defeat the other venoms combining their kung fu. Ho knows the lizard style, but Yang knows all five of the venom styles. It is because of their bond that they can defeat the evil clan members and prevail.

THE FIVE DEADLY VENOMS

BLOOD BROTHERS

"More often Zhang replaces romance with male bonding, producing a series of smoldering masculine couples" (Bordwell 250). Women were not commonly seen in Chang's films; usually they were background characters who showed up as entertainers at a bar or for the General. When there was a female role that was more than just entertainment, she usually caused the breakup of the brotherhood. In **BLOOD BROTHERS**, Mi Lan is Huang's wife, but Chang is his sworn brother. We are never told how they became brothers; the main point is that we know that they just are. The two of them do spend more time with each other than Huang does with his wife; he rarely spends time with her at all. Huang would rather go to the clubs and meet other women than be with his own wife.

As I talked about before, an affair ensues between Ma Hsin and Mi Lan. This was the ultimate downfall for the brotherhood of Chang and Huang. When Chang tried to tell Huang the truth, he accused him of being jealous and attacked him. After Huang was killed by Ma Hsin's men the brotherhood was over, it ended because her.

The thirteen brothers in **THE HEROIC ONES** were also broken up by a woman. When they go to assassinate the opposing general, they hide out in a woman's home. Brother's Four and Twelve during the night went and attempted to rape the girl. Xiao came at the right moment and stopped them from performing the crime. This in turn made them even more hateful of Xiao, and of the other generals as well because they did not stick up for them. Granted what the two brothers were attempting was very wrong, it's still a fact that the woman inadvertently broke down the brotherhood.

The theme of brotherhood also develops the emotions of characters to explore the make-up of a hero. A hero is a very vague term that means something different to everyone, but Chang's films give a more definitive definition of what a hero is. In Chang's films, a hero is someone who will do anything for his brother, even if it means giving up his own life.

For example, in **THE HEROIC ONES**, Shih Ching Szu (Ti Lung) stands to fight the elite guard alone and tells the others to leave. He knows that there is a good chance that he would die in the situation, but he doesn't care. All that matters to him is that his brothers get away safely. Chang's heroes are very much knight-errant because of their courage in the face of death. These characters are heroes because they show loyalty to their brothers, and have no fear to sacrifice it all for them.

Chang Cheh's films are easily recognizable by the style that the action is filmed. There is a distinct formula that is used in nearly every fight sequence in his films. When he has a fight sequence, he showcases every aspect of the fight, whether it's hand to hand combat or with weapons.

One of the biggest distinctions of a Chang Cheh fight sequence is that the majority of the fights are very long, extravagant, and beautifully choreographed. "In terms of action, it is not enough to have action in a scene -- the action must be powerful and contain aesthetic beauty, the shots must carry the motion" (Chang Cheh). Each fight seems like a story unto itself; there is a beginning, middle, and an end to it. Usually the fight will start off with the two sides confronting each other about a conflict. Then they will engage each other in combat fight for awhile, and then one side will win. But there are elements that will make them a little story on their own. Take for example a fight scene near the beginning of **BLOOD BROTHERS**. Huang and Chang get ambushed by Governmental soldiers. They fight valiantly for awhile, but the soldiers trap them, then Ma Hsin arrives in time to save them. This could be seen as the last minute rescue made famous by D.W. Griffith, which would usually happen at the end to resolve the movie. This is just one example out of many in the mini stories portrayed in Chang's action scenes.

The fights themselves are also very distinct. Whether the actors used their fists or weapons, it was very fast paced, but every move was seen. A lot of fight sequences done by other directors are also long and fast, but not everything is shown. You can hear the swords clanging, but you didn't see the swords hit. That doesn't happen in Chang's films, there is a move for every sound effect used and you see the move clearly.

Another thing Chang does in his fights is showcase the talents of the actors. His fight sequences are the opposite of fights filmed now. Instead of using extreme close-ups and using an edit after every move, he takes medium and long range shots so you see the fluidity of the action and the style of kung fu used. Instead of cutting every time the action moves out of the frame, he will use a tracking shot so we don't miss a move. By showing the fight sequence in its entirety, it not only shows the flow of the action but it showcases the actor's talents in martial arts. Watching one of Chang's fights you never question if the person fighting on screen is a stunt double or the actual actor. The majority of times that an edit occurs, the next frame will be a close-up of the actor starting his attack. Instead of cutting to a wide angle shot of the fight, Chang always zooms out to a medium shot and lets the fight ensue. Because he chooses to zoom instead of cut we know for a fact that the person fighting is the actor playing the part.

Another signature of a Chang Cheh film is the overemphasis of blood and death. During a fight the hero might get wounded and immediately blood would be all over his body, but this wouldn't stop him from fighting. After getting injured it drove the hero more into battle frenzy and he would take out as many of the enemies that he could

before he himself was killed. The death of either the hero or one of the soldiers is always portrayed as a giant spectacle. When someone is killed, they just don't fall down and go limp. Instead you see the pain in their faces, you hear their cry. Then they might stagger around and try to kill some more of the enemy, or they might just fall down and roll until their final spasm that would signify their death. It's almost as if the characters death is the most important part of their life so they have to make it as big as possible.

One way that Chang was able to put all of these recurring themes in his films is because he wrote the scripts for the majority of his films. This helps make him an auteur because he's not just taking someone else's script and putting it on the screen. He came up with the ideas for the storylines and how to make his characters pursue the themes of brotherhood and deception. Even without doing this he would still be considered an auteur because of the recurring themes and style.

Finally, the last component that makes Chang an auteur is he continually used the same actors in his films which further enhanced this role of brotherhood. His two main teams were that of David Chiang and Ti Lung, and the group of five known as the Venoms, they got the name due to **THE FIVE DEADLY VENOMS**. Since they made multiple films together we were able to see them form brotherhoods film after film. Although the films and characters were different, the theme was still the same.

Chang Cheh was a director who became an auteur. The films he made had recurring themes, and they also were very definable by the style in which he filmed. He also furthered his auteur status by writing his own scripts, and by using the same actors film after film. His films were some of the greatest of their time, and still are to this day. He was an influence for filmmakers during his time and for the generation after him and will forever be an influence as long as films are made.

BREAKING POINT

Bo Arne Vibenius's Fuck All Exploration of A Sick Mind as essayed
by David Zuzelo

*Bo Arne Vibenius made very few films, but will certainly be remembered for his masterwork of SwedeSleaze **THRILLER-EN GRYM FILM** (They Call Her One Eye, Hooker's Revenge)... but that film had a bizarre release history that left it's director angry, cut out like a whore's eyeball and ready to unleash a new film on unsuspecting Swedish censors.*

But as with much of his career, things weren't going to turn out as planned. **BREAKING POINT** (Pornografisk Thriller) is anything but average, a full out assault on the viewers perceptions and reactions, it stands tall as a surreal and occasionally silly thriller, but when you add in the punishing conditions it was made under, this may be the film that Vibenius will leave behind as his personal powerhouse. Sadly it is not an easy film to locate, and nobody seems to be looking anymore. Even the director has no access to a decent element...so what the fuck is **BREAKING POINT**. Swedish sin from a director that tapped his darkest reflections, deeper than anything "Alex Fridolinski" could dig up for **THRILLER**.

Opening on a sinister looking eye watching an elevator

fall in a darkened hall, we jump cut to a woman in the supermarket. Already the audience knows the mundane everyday world of shopping and carrying groceries is about to be destroyed. Oh, and it is. Brutally attacked by an unseen assailant, the opening salvo contains forced coupling and visceral bludgeoning violence.

The first word of the film is uttered as we meet our "protagonist" Bob Bellings at work. An unassuming presence at his office desk, Bellings checks and stamps papers with a grim robotic precision and a shiny donut glaze haze in his eyes. Those same eyes light up as a woman passes by however and he only says one thing. A word that is obviously important to him.

"Bitch."

Obviously, this guy has a problem with women.

Bob watches as a news broadcast talks of the rape and violence perpetrated by some "bastard illegal citizen" (according to the police officer being interviewed) and alternates dreamily between watching the women in the office, trying to demolish them with his eyes and staring down his female coworkers as the television gives the ladies of Stockholm some advice that I don't think is very sound.

"Keep calm and let him do what he wants. Worse comes to worse you'll only get raped."

A "well researched" statistic that 89 percent of women have rape fantasies is dropped in for a moment of mad science and is even interpreted by the televised talking heads into the idea that the rapist is simply giving most women what they want...but the cops do request that he stop killing them!

BREAKING POINT, it's not exactly a feminist tract.

The women of the office flirt with Bob right after this is "fact" is reverberating through his demented brainpan, because in this film NOTHING gets a woman horny like rape talk. Well, at least 89 percent of them. Bob cannot process this sensual attention and instead of lust taking over for Bob he expresses the only reaction he seems ca-

pable of, which is rage of course. He takes this feeling with him away from the office and into the streets. More stalking, more raping ensues.

"Undress you."

However, the rapes become carnal events as the women give into Bellings-allowing him to kiss the semen from their faces after he is finished with them. The world of Bob Bellings is becoming sicker than his mind is it would appear. So, he adjusts his fantasy world accordingly, re-running the rapes again in strange sequences that involve flies landing on penises to be painfully flicked off and a bit of improper gunplay.

Amidst all these afternoon activities, he spends time alone at home, building model trains and fantasizing intently on his post job antics. Is Bob reverting, letting his inner child free in his sexual fantasy world? Or is he really a deranged rapist?

The women that Bob encounters during the day are a weird bunch and he can't seem to take his aggression out while there, so he goes a passive aggressive route that seems all too fitting. Yep, by masturbating into a cup and spiking the coffee of a woman that beats him down (at least verbally). His plan is thwarted as she adjusts to the taste and, of course, enjoys it. More rage and venting on those outside the crippling job and endless office that traps Bob occurs.

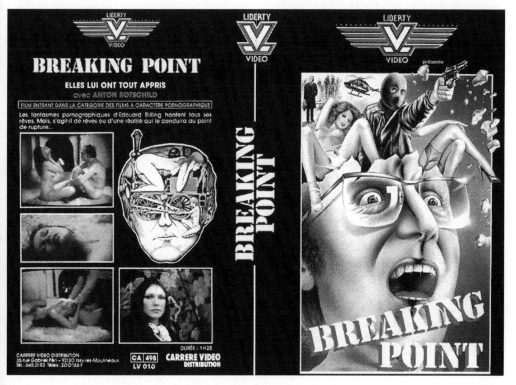

37

And now dear readers, things get weird!

Televised talkers inform us that a new law has been passed in Sweden...all citizens MUST carry a gun! Woah, if only Christina Lindberg had known this prior to **THRILLER-A CRUEL PICTURE**!! To become involved in the Swedish Wild West all you have to do is go pick up your hammer of doom at any weapons shop. So Bob does just that, and he also takes some police issue "fragmentation" ammo from a rabid gun dealer who wants to see the streets "cleaned up." After a few test shots that leave trees felled all about we now have Ballistic and Pugilistic to the pussy that imperils him, a deadlier Bob Bellings.

And then he picks up a child... and I'll leave it to you to see what happens. Gripping and a rare moment of reprieve for the viewer await. Of course Bob also encounters a woman who wants to fuck his gearshift, literally, before he is randomly kidnapped by robbers. Shifting gears with the still drying fluids on it, **BREAKING POINT** suddenly becomes an action film... and the whole experience unravels until the final twist is revealed. Bellings is shown for exactly what he is and the audience is left to either scratch their heads or be left in awe. Now we are left to gather what is real, imagined and wished for in each and every scene of coupling carnage.

Did I mention that the gang of thugs that Bellings must deal with speaks in a completely demented Tough Talk version of English? The JIVE MOTHERS are super fucking badass!

Bo Arne Vibenius' **BREAKING POINT** started life as a completely different project. After the disappointing returns of **THRILLER-A CRUEL PICTURE**, a film that Vibenius and his dedicated crew poured an immense amount of work into, the film maker was looking to try again with AB Audiovisual to create something just as unique and unrelenting to get audiences riled up. To understand the disappointment of **THRILLER** to its director you have to understand that he felt undermined by AIP licensing the picture and editing it down to **THEY CALL HER ONE EYE**. There were monetary issues by Vibenius' account, but that-like much of the director's career, that is probably open to some speculation. Needless to say, he went into his new project with a new vigor to create and control his own work. It just needed to be a commercial success...

THRILLER-A CRUEL PICTURE was "commercial" according to Vibenius, and he wanted to take his formula further. Well, the chance fell apart as the new film was to be partially financed by the government of Sweden using a money matching program with private funds. When, at the last moment, financing fell apart Vibenius and crew were forced to scramble something together! **THRILLER-A CRUEL PICTURE** was created very quickly and the writing process was described by Bo Arne in the following manner. "My fingers were actually bleeding after those three days OF NOT ONLY MENTAL BUT ALSO PHYSICAL FINGER WORK!" Fueled by nervous energy and the unending desire to film something...anything... with the government grant and the script was pounded out in two days. That is faster than **THRILLER**. Fingers are bleeding and this Porno FutureShock was the result. Poured straight up from the stressed out psyche, **BREAKING POINT** was ready to be filmed.

Vibenius was very lucky to have his talented Director of Photography, Andreas Bellis, agree to take up the lead role. Bellis has worked as a cinematographer for many years including a run with Greek CineManiac Niko Mastorakis and is a huge part of both **THRILLER** and Vibenius' personal success. Luckily he also had another large, yet mostly hidden, talent in his pants and he would be willing to flaunt and flog it with style...even pausing to flick a fly off the head of that Potatiskorv. Bellis is excellent in the film-lifting it up (or down as the case may be) into dementia even during the sequences that stretch past surreal and wipe out into a land of bizarre bullets and evil jive mothafuckin' thugs.

Truly an odd film worth investigation by a sleaze seeker, **BREAKING POINT** is an important piece in the hard to finish puzzle of Bo Arne Vibenius' cinema. **BREAKING POINT**'s harrowed "hero" cum rapist cum adventurer slash fantasizer, Bob Bellings, definitely feels like an avatar for a man that can't seem to get what he wants-no matter how he works for it nor how worthy his talents are. At the end of the film when Bellings utters the line "Nothing ever happens in this shitty town" the frustration is palpable. In 2000 I had the chance to sit down with Bo Arne Vibenius and viewing this was an odd experience for sure. I had no idea what to expect and it was a really riveting experience. Just as Bellings used his time away from his family in the film to immerse himself in a strange fantasy (or blurry reality), he comes crashing back to humdrum reality-so must it be to come off of making a film that those responsible pin all of their hopes upon, yet never reach the success they feel they deserve.

BREAKING POINT is mired in Pseudonyms. Vibenius chose a different set of nom de plumes with the interesting use of "Stan Kowalski"-the brutal every day man of "A Streetcar Named Desire". It fits very much with Bob Bellings... After his turn as "Hot Dog Vendor" in **THRILLER**, look for Vibenius as "Police Inspector Dan Clark" who curses out "that bastard of an unauthorized citizen!" Other names that ring out with ironic humor include Adam de Loup, Adolf Deutch, Urban Hitler (!) and TURBOman on stunt driving. These names aside, the film has a very good cast. Sex starlet Barbro Klingered appears as "The Woman" that torments Bob, and certainly doesn't shy away from some strong sequences that include guns with condoms and gear shift sex. And re-appearing from **THRILLER** is Per-Axel Arosenius, who has an interesting story. After running afoul of the Swedish Taxation office he protested by setting himself on fire in front of the offices in Nacka. Another strange ending in the Vibenius story...

BREAKING POINT also bears the distinction of having Anton Karras playing of the famous ditty from **THE THIRD MAN**, The Harry Lime Theme, here re-interpolated into the "Head Theme" in the films credits by the ever brilliant Ralph Lundsten. **BREAKING POINT** is aurally the equal of **THRILLER-A CRUEL PICTURE**. Dementedly reactive to the images of the film, Lundsten adds a complete dimension with his sound and score presentation. According to the composer and director, Anton Karas arrived at Lundsten's studio with his Zither and played his most famous song a few times. And that was it. However, those few takes form the basis of the weird score that will stick in your head. Forget Harry Lime, I don't need him...Bob Bellings I'll never forget.

Filmed in Stockholm and released in 1975-and again banned by Swedish Censors outright, you have to see this one to believe it. The limited Swedish release is unfortunate, and Vibenius claims the film had a very long and profitable run in France where it was released by Impex Films, which means there must be more elements somewhere in the world than the often duplicated and boot-legged Swedish VHS print. While I have never seen paperwork regarding any kind of masters, Vibenius told us that he lost the film elements to an unscrupulous New York City distributor many years ago. That should be a hurdle to overcome for any interested licensor!

Also, if you are in Stockholm and feel like visiting one of the famous buildings in the film, Bob Bellings works at the Werner-Gren Institute... check it out. Just don't drink the coffee!

Making a fantastic cult film and watching it wade in obscurity for decades was a life changing event for Bo Arne Vibenius... and when it does come back to the mainstream consciousness, I'm sure that is just as difficult. Recently **THRILLER** received a theatrical showing in Sweden. As someone that feels kind of close to the film and the man behind it (though he would probably just as soon fling me off a roof as speak to me), it made me a bit sad to hear that he did not attend. His children did, and that makes me think of **BREAKING POINT** all the more. Bo Arne Vibenius is a true talent, and a singular one at that, but I believe that his Bob Bellings is very present, if not real. While his legacy may not consist of many films, **BREAKING POINT** is a high water mark of Swedish Sinning in the Cinema. Seek it out. Now. Worse comes to worse...only your eyes will be raped!

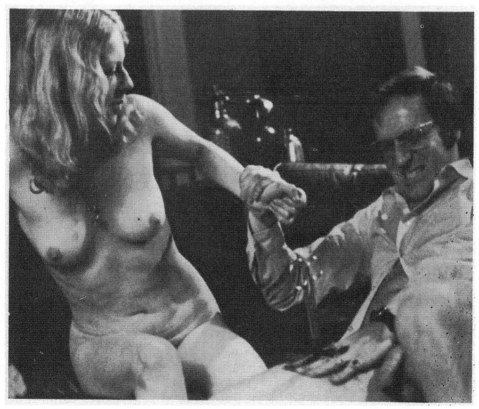

THE PINK BEYOND:

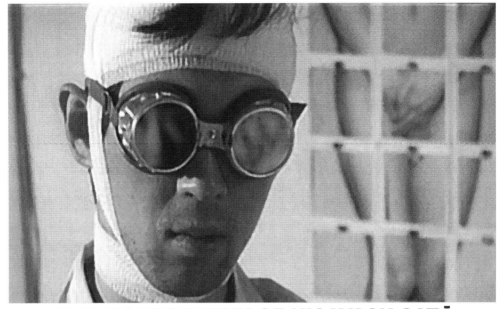

THE ICONOGRAPHY OF HISAYASU SATŌ
By Jason Meredith

White static on a TV-screen… rolling images of women in torment… an antagonist hiding behind the viewfinder of a small home video camera… images way to familiar to the observant audience of the films of Pinku director Hisayasu Satō.

At the start of the nineties, the Japanese Pinku genre was in turmoil. The largest producer of the genre, Nikkatsu went bust, the smaller studio's where struggling, legendary directors had made their last few important movies and the new kids on the block where breaking new ground and genre conventions. Just like American slasher movies have a formula that they follow, there's a set prefix for number of sex scenes for the Pinku genre. Perhaps these restraints where exactly what was needed to refuel the creative visions of Pinku directors, as despite the genre slowly fading into oblivion, it wouldn't quite die. The directors later to be known as "The Four Heavenly Kings of Pink" – Kazuhiro Sano, Toshiki Satō, Takahisa Zeze, and Hisayasu Satō - never looked back at formula or tradition. Armed with a seize the day mentality, they broke new ground, cutting back on sex scenes, introducing new darker themes, pushing the boundaries for onscreen violence, and preparing the Pinku genre for the coming next millennium.

Making his debut in 1985 with **GEKIAI! LOLITA MITSURO** *(Distorted Sense of Touch aka Mad Love! Lolita Poaching)*, Hisayasu Satō has been an effective and highly productive director of Pinku films, exploring, satirizing and at times aiming critique with the almost sixty titles he's directed since then. Films containing eroticism, warped revenge, masochism, sadism, bestiality, and then there's the area which perhaps makes him somewhat unique in the Pinku genre, the ease with which he shifted from heterosexual Pinku to homosexual

PINKU: KURUTTA BUTOKAI (Muscle aka Lunatic Theatre) 1988 and **KAMEN NO YUWAKU** (Temptation of the Mask) 1987 are prime examples of how Satō shifts his narrative and subject is designated to a gay themes. These films are also of importance to the survival of the genre, as they also saw the shitenno come together for the first time. Just like generic Japanese cinema, the Pinku genre holds a long tradition of apprenticeships and learning under the wings of an older master of the arts. Satō came through the guidance of amongst others Yōjirô Takita, and has in his own turn mentored the likes of **SHINJI IMAOKA OF ONNA NO KAPPA** (Underwater Love) 2011 fame. **TEMPTATION OF THE MASK** saw Takahasi Zeze as Satō 's assistant director and through this collaboration came the casting of Kazuhiro Satō, who later on would turn to directing and also become one of the Four Heavenly Kings of Pink.

Watching the movies of Hisayasu Satō there are several themes, traits and an iconography that becomes an apparent pattern to reading his works, and within these traits is where you can read the subtext of his movies.

Voyeurism is a huge part of Satō's universe. Repeatedly there will be characters watching video footage either of sexual acts, their own sexual conquests, or even working in the industry, which is shown through the camera. The cabdriver antagonist [Isao Nonaka] in **HITOZUMA KOREKUTÂ** (Wife Collector) 1985, videotapes his rape victims and has a large collection of perverted home movies in his torture chamber. **NUSUMIDORI REPORT: INSHA!** (Turtle Vision) 1991, sees Eiji [Kouichi Imaizumi], in a guerilla filmmaking style, shooting prostitutes as they fuck their customers in back alleys. Tapes he later sells to a pornographer that makes money off the hooker's candid sex. **ABUNÔRAMU INGYAKI** (Re-Wind, aka Celluloid Nightmares) 1988, tells the tale of Satō regular, Kiyomi Ito, obsessing over the distorted images she's seen on a snuff tape. The creation of these tapes becomes an important sub-plot in the main narrative. The futuristically themed **NEKKEDDU BURÂDDO: MAGAKYU** (Splatter: Naked Blood) 1996, even takes the voyeurism into the point of view in cyberspace. Lulu [Norie Yasui] and Ayano [Mayu Sakuma] both work in the adult industry in Satō's latest movie **NAMAE NO NAI ONNA-TACHI** (Love & Loathing and Lulu & Ayano) 2010, and there's a repeated use of viewfinder images to separate reality from staged film set reality. Believe it or not, but Satō's latest film is also one that aims critique towards the J.A.V. industry! The examples are many, and the voyeuristic theme that taps right into our basic mannerisms as human beings. We all want to know what is happening behind the closed door, and sneak a peak at forbidden subject matter.

The dark themes and violent rapes found in Satō's work, and others, may at first seem to be sensationalistic content – which according to genre convention is demanded – but especially in Satō's films the violence and rape are metaphors for destruction, a disassembly of communication,

and a critique towards Japanese society. Characters rarely have much of a social network, but instead are tormented by their social alienation. Splendid examples of this can be found in Satō's naming of his movies, (Pinku films often become retitled after playing the Pinku cinemas and also when reissued on video/DVD) such as **WIFE COLLECTOR** which originally was titled ROTTEN CITY. One can obviously find the same metaphors in certain moments of his movies, such as the shocking scene in **SPLATTER: NAKED BLOOD** where Yukima Hayashi armed with knife and fork slowly, but with determination dismembers her own body slicing off and eating her own nipple, labia and finally eyeball. Memorable to say the least!

A recurrent trait that you will find in Satō's films is main characters acting or running through streets and back alleys whilst surprised on lookers react in shock… or in the most disturbing moments, with apathy. This is the guerilla style street photography that Satō refers to as "The Sledgehammer Technique", and it's all about shooting violent, provocative or disturbing scenes without any permits what so ever. In these existing locations, innocent by-passers become involuntary extras and their reactions to the actions almost read as a social reflection on the people of Japan.

Take the ending of **RE-WIND** which see's Kiyomi Ito running from a razor wielding maniac though a busy streets of Shibuya. Or my favorite "Sledgehammer" moment, found in **WIFE COLLECTOR** where Isao Nonaka has kidnapped a young woman, has a makeshift gas chamber in the back of his cab, where he sedates his female victim with gas before he videotapes and rapes her in the back of the car as it nonchalantly stands parked in at the side of a heavily trafficked stretch of motorway. A climactic moment in **MIBÔJIN HENTAI JIGOKU** (Widow's Perverted Hell) 1991 sees Yuri Hime naked as nature intended bound in chains, in the middle of the street begging the passing people to help her masturbate! Wham, feel the punch of the Sledgehammer. Taken out of their context, the scenes all seem like sinister passages perfect for luring in a gullible audience searching for a smut fest, but if you follow the narrative to this point of the movie, they all tap into an important trait of the cinema of Satō.

A predominate Satō trait is what I call "obsessive revenge fetish" In the major part of Satō's movies there is clear

刺青

SI-SEI

私の体が
それを受け入れる…

原作 谷崎潤一郎

青井怜
弓削智久

谷崎文学、禁断のエロティシズム

ping, Sadism, Voyeurism); Misaki [Naomi Haigo who went on to star in Kazu Komizu's **SHOJO NO HAR-AWATA** (Entrails of a Virgin) after **WIFE COLLECTOR**] has her rape/degradation fetish seen so clearly in the way she seeks perilous sexual encounters. Random sexual encounters with strangers generate emotions equal of those Isao provoked with his previous assault. (The Obsessive Revenge Fetish) Misaki's younger sister Akkio [Minako Ogawa] has her own fetishes too, namely Misaki and a rape obsession! Akkio is stalking her sister and photographing her sexual exploits. The lust that these images stir in her indicate that she too wants to be assaulted like her sister and be accepted as a woman. This can be read into the movie through a steamy lovemaking session with her doll. She's prepared to move on from being a child, a symbolic subplot that is enhanced when she later hangs the same doll she earlier made love to. She wants the same experience that Misaki had so that she can become an adult woman.

Themes and fetishes that all come together in perfect harmony, hooking into each other just like Velcro, and all with a deeper meaning. So keep this in mind the next time you watch a Pinku movie directed by Satō, The Heavenly King of Pink, because the images are not merely there for your voyeuristic kicks or to satisfy your lust for smut, Hisayasu Satō is actually trying to tell you something.

storyline which concerns seeking out a former antagonist to seek closure in the depraved acts committed against the protagonist. The twist being that they are not after revenge, but rather to relive the experience! When Satō utilizes his "obsessive revenge fetish" it's a clear nod of the hat to his admiration for Italian director Pier Paolo Pasolini. Trough the sadism of the sexual rituals, torture and torment his protagonists endure, they find reunification, new strength, and they become closer finally finding the closure they have been looking for throughout the movie. Just like Pasolini's **TEOREMA** 1968, - later reworked by Takashi Miike as **BIJITÂ Q** (Visitor Q) 2001 – there is order to be found through provocation and chaos. **MUSCLE** also features several homages to Pasolini, as Ryuzaki [Takeshi Ito] searches for his protagonist Kitami [Simon Kumai] in the art-house cinema screening Pasolini's **PORCILE** (Pigpen) 1969– despite Kitami cutting off and stealing Ryuzaki's arm which he keeps preserved in a jar of formaldehyde, talk about an obsessive revenge fetish! In the same movie, Satō repeatedly uses British industrial band Throbbing Gristle's Pasolini homage **OSTIA** (The Death of Pasolini) on the soundtrack, as a theme for the movie.

The theme Satō uses the most is fetishes. Characters in Satō's universe all have fixed fetishes that tap into each other and even other characters and their fetishes. One fetish will hook onto another and lead to a third and so on, in an almost never-ending circle. A fabulous example of this is to be found in **WIFE COLLECTOR**. Isao has his rape/voyeurism fetish, which drives him to his acts (Kidnap-

42

ROLL DEM BONES!

Or How I Spent a Week's Grocery Money on Indian Monster Movies and Didn't live to regret it.
by Tim Paxton

INTRODUCTION TO MY OBSESSION

Balancing the need for food with the want of watching a batch of unknown horror films can be a delicate matter. You know, nourishment for body vs. that of the soul. Tough call. Major case-in-point: making out the grocery list for the week and surfing the web simultaneously. Need potatoes (*check*), celery (*check*), **JAANI DUSHMAN** (*check*), cat food (*check*).... oh hell, looks like about fifteen VCDs and DVDs just fell into the shopping cart.

Again with the conundrum: eating well for a week or watching an armful of never before seen DVDs and VCDs that I know absolutely nothing about? $100 can buy a lot of weird films. Hmmm, the basement *is* pretty well stocked with shelves of post-apocryphal canned goods.

I've shopped at a lot of different web sites over the past 15 years. I've seen a lot come and go. I used to buy bucket loads of Hong Kong VCDs thru bluelaser.com & DVDs from sensasian.com. Both companies have since closed shop. There is ethaicd.com, but I seem to have burned through their catalog pretty quickly. So, for nothing better to do with my time for the past two years I have shopped at induna.com, which is where I found this month's stash.

So what can $100 get you from induna.com? More than you can imagine despite the hellacious cost of overseas shipping from Calcutta, India to Northeastern Ohio, US of A. Most of what I purchased were VCDs rather than DVDs (primarily because VCDs are still very popular in India, and few of the choice titles are yet to be available on DVD). VCDs are the digital equivalent to VHS video tapes recorded at the SLP (six hour) mode. For those of you who never experienced looking at grainy video tape, a good comparison are some of the "4-on-1" DVDs that companies like Mill Creek produce for their "100 Best Whatever" series. With Indian VCDs it's not just horrible picture quality but there are no options for English subtitles or extras that are usually found on most DVDs. Let's not forget to mention that a great deal of the source material for these VCDS are cruddy VHS tapes.

You can't polish a turd.

So why blow a week's worth of food on a pile of VCDs? The films, man, the films. Most of what I purchased are the oddball shit-productions most fans and critics of "psychotronic cinema" wouldn't touch if you paid them.

The best part about receiving a large bundle or two of VCDs and DVDs in the mail is sitting thru ALL of them. Yes,

exploitation goodies like terror, violence, and monstrous entities and you have very yourself a very profitable commodity.

The fact that these films are still being made today, albeit with a slicker look (that, sadly, apes more popular Western exploitation), is due to the lower cost of digital production. If you need some grounding; a far-fetched analogy for the West would be to compare the last thirty years of Indian exploitation cinema to that of the U.S. Grindhouse market that fed small theaters and the drive-in circuit during the 1950s-80s. This was an exciting powerhouse of filmmaking that thrived before the rise of multiplexes, video sales, theatre consolidation, and cable TV crippled the industry.

For the sake of sanity, length, and simplicity this article will not, with one major exception, deal with any of the films made by the prolific Ramsay family. F.U. Ramsay and his sons Tulsi, Shyam, Kiran, Kumar, and Gangu Ramsay took the traditional idea of Indian horror and married it with the thrills of western fright films. Productions from "The House of Ramsay" are better made than most of what will be covered hereafter. Six of their films have had major DVD releases from Mondo Macabro, and should be in the collection of any self-made exploitation junkie: **PURANA MANDIR, BANDH DARWAZA, MAHAKAAL, TAHKHANA, VEERANA,** and **PURANI HAVELI**.

even when they're the infamous "Grade C" "A Certificate" horror films primarily from the film industry of Southern India[1]. South Indian cinema covers Kannada, Malayalam, Tamil, Telugu, Tulu and Konkani. To be honest, I can't distinguish the spoken languages, so I couldn't tell you which film was from what region (although most seemed to be dubbed into Hindi).

The infamous "Grade C" is not just for the horror genre. Other exploitative genres include jungle adventures, action-adventure, and just plain old sexploitation. According to a 2007 survey, over 150 C-grade films are made in Mumbai alone (not accounting for the Southern films), most for pennies when compared to their mainstream counterparts (typically $20,000 to $60,000). However, after the paltry theatrical showings, the majority of the profit comes from primarily the sale of VCDs[2]. The Indian Censor Board passes them with an A Certificate, but usually they're shown the 'clean' version. The 'real' reels are inserted later at the single-screen theaters, dingy video parlors, movie tents, video cars on small trains, and so forth. These alternative reels typically introduce nudity and softcore sex sequences. Add the additional

The Ramsays were a pivotal powder keg in the development of Indian horror films from the early 70s until the end of the 80s. It was their films and their approach to horror that opened the floodgates for other films in the genre. Noted author Pete Tombs sums up the all-important element of these movies that I love: *"These rules have held fast pretty much up to the present day. Filmmakers who have chosen to ignore them have done so at their peril. Subtlety and originality aren't the order of the day here. Indian audiences expect their horror to be direct and up front. The films must have a monster and the monster must look gruesome. Filmmakers talk about the concept of a "horror face", meaning that the evil within the creature must be outwardly visible."*[3]

THE BEASTS

Some of my favorite Indian monster movies include those that feature huge lumbering demons and devils (often referred to as "ghosts" in the films). They shuffle and stomp about with a stiff but powerful gait, yet they somehow are able to catch their human prey who are madly scampering away from them (what I call "Kharis-effect" of the Universal Pictures 1940s' shambling mummy movies). They are large

1 Pete Tombs, *"The Beast From Bollywood: a history of the Indian horror film,"* Fear Without Frontiers: Horror Cinema Across The Globe, ed. Steven Jay Schneider (FAB Press, 2003) 243-253.
2 This information may be in dispute, but after some research thru online Indian film journals and blogs these figures come pretty close for that year, and I assume you can extrapolate for any additional years.

3 Pete Tombs, *"The Beast From Bollywood: a history of the Indian horror film,"* Fear Without Frontiers: Horror Cinema Across The Globe, ed. Steven Jay Schneider (FAB Press, 2003) 243-253.

and hairy. Gorilla hairy. Actually, more like *gorilla costume hairy* as most of the creature effects are store-bought rubber masks and monkey outfits with visible zippers.

Their appearance could quite possibly be a cinematic/cultural aspect derived from religious theatre (not unlike Chinese horror films and Peking Opera). It could also be that trotting down to the local costume stop and picking up a few rubber masks it is the least expensive way to produce a monster in a hurry. An early example of this ape monster appears in 1963 when Mohammad Hussain made his King Kong-influenced giant ape jungle film **SHIKARI**. Hirsute creatures also have also performed in mythological movies, as in the immensely entertaining **BAJRANG BALI** from 1976. In that film, besides the less-than-hairy form of Lord Hanuman and his fellow demi-god apes, there is a *vanara* (monkey-man) called Kalpa. Again, sadly, not all that impressive looking.

Prior to the popularity of international ghost and monster based horror films that were often based off of **FRIDAY THE 13TH, THE EVIL DEAD, HALLOWEEN,** and **THE RING**, horror movies were not seen as decent entertainment for the masses. The few ghost films that *did* surface in the 1950s and 60s were low-key affairs, often dealing with reincarnation or haunted mansions played for laughs. Or, as in the 1951 thriller **JIGHANSA**, it was a "Scooby Doo" affair as the seven-foot monster was shown to be a man attacking folks in disguise. Any truly phantasmagorical movie outside of the occasional fantastic "mythological-devotional" or fantasy/comedy production was a rarity. Although, from what I can figure out, there seems to be more of a tradition of mystery and horror in southern film.

However, the Hindi-language 1979 "werewolf" monster movie **JAANI DUSHMAN** caught a lot of viewers off guard. Although banned outright by censors, the film is full of all the essential horror elements one that would later be put to good use by the Ramsays (but with a lot less budget, mediocre songs, stolen scores, and less-than-stellar stars and starlets).

In the film a young man discovers that his bride-to-be has cheated on him, and in his anger he turns into an entity full of hate and kills his wife and her lover. But the fun doesn't stop there as the huge hairy monster murders one bride-to-be after another, gleefully chasing and dispatching the screaming woman with a roar and a leer. The film is full of the usual red herrings as one villager is suspected of being the monster and then another. Just as it seems that all is lost, the lumbering creature is discovered in an underground temple[4] and after a fierce battle is run thru with a holy trident.

JAANI DUSHMAN was a very important horror film for Hindu director Rajkumar Kohli, who no doubt was cashing in on his earlier supernatural snake-goddess thriller called **NAGIN** (1976). Both films were initially banned by the Indian government due to their content, although the songs from **JAANI DUSHMAN** were major hits. Nevertheless, Kohli tried his hand at the genre again with the excellent ghost tale **BEES SAAL BAAD** in 1988, but fell flat on his face when his update of **JAANI DUSHMAN** (incorporating elements from **NAGIN**) crashed and burned upon release in 2002.

While **JANNI DUSHMAN** was a horror film, it was still one made for the "upper class". When the Ramsay's introduced their monsters, they followed a newly profitable set of rules: " *Firstly, that horror movies are generally low budget affairs. Secondly, that they follow Western models very closely with the "Indian" elements more or less grafted onto a generic plot. Thirdly, that the exploitable elements of horror make it unnecessary to have either great music or star casts; and finally, that they will be most popular with rural audiences and the urban poor and treated as rather a joke by everyone else.*"[5]

4 For the longest time I believed that all the underground temples and palaces in Indian films were fictionalized places of hyper and hoary imaginations. Nope. They are not that uncommon. A good read can be found in ARCHAEOLOGY Magazine, Volume 64 Number 3, May/June 2011, "India's Underground Water Temples" by Samir S. Patel.

5 Pete Tombs, *"The Beast From Bollywood: a history of the Indian horror film,"* Fear Without Frontiers: Horror Cinema Across The Globe, ed. Steven Jay Schneider (FAB Press, 2003) 243-253.

Information about these productions from the lower depth of the India film industry has been slowly rising to the top of the internet as more and more of the film are released on VCD (and sometimes DVD) and appear on YouTube. The overt sleaziness of these largely independent productions is the major attraction for most film fans. However contrary to their own rule of the "horror face", Tulsi and Shyam Ramsay crafted a 1991 whimsical and fun albeit violent monster movie musical for kids called **AJOOBA KUDRAT KAA**. The film is paced rather well, and there are some charming musical numbers, yet as a late entry into the genre, the film lacks any real horror elements other than a rampaging monster. Most notable is the six minute opus "Yeti We Love You" sung by a little girl to her big hairy goofball of a friend: the Yeti, a bumbling monster that has already slaughtered at least four people.

So what is this kid doing frolicking in the snowy mountains of India? Northern India is home to the Himalayas, with peaks over 20,000 feet. Not only does it snow there, but it snows every month of the year, with peaks covered in glaciers. That's where the Yeti comes in (considered by Lord Hanuman devotees a direct descendant of The Monkey God himself). The young girl, Sasha by name, is the daughter of a forest ranger who works in that region. She is kidnapped by some nasty gangsters who want to ransom her back to Ranger and his sassy wife. The girl escapes and encounters the Yeti who is a friendly, dog-faced monster who is peaceful and kind at heart, despite crushing the skulls of some men in the opening sequence of the film.

AJOOBA KUDRAT KAA ("The Magnificent Guardian"), as far as I can tell, is only available for purchase on VCD or for viewing on YouTube. It appears as if the Ramsays spent time making the monster somewhat believable. They did a pretty good job, although the Yeti still ambles after its prey in that shambling gait popular with Indian monster movies. Any second the poor actor in the creature suit is going to land face first in the snow.

Taking a mighty step down in production we find ourselves hip-deep in the delightful muck of sleazy "Grade C" epics. Not that **AJOOBA KUDRAT KAA** isn't part of that extended family, but compared to the next batch of films, the Yeti epic is the wealthy uncle.

Welcome to the likes of **PYASA SHAITAN** (1978/87?), **DAFAN** (2001) and **PYAASA HAIWAN** (2003). These films make up a trilogy of tat: very entertaining cheapness. It is in these types of films that we are introduced to the most sordid of cinematic hirsute humanoids ever to mutilate, rape and kill mankind[6].

Joginder Shelly's **PYASA SHAITAN** ("Thirsty Devil") is a composite mishmash made from an older Malayalam film called **VAYANADAN THAMPAN** (1978) to which the director of **PYASA SHAITAN** gleefully added his own footage. The end result is a crazy psychedelic horror film that spins out of control, whipping us back and forth through an insane amount of visual elements. The film opens by directly "borrowing" the demonic forest rape scene from Sam Raimi's **THE EVIL DEAD**, and plopping it down in Indian horror territory. A woman is molested by light rays from a flying hairy demon-guru who chatters and screams non-stop in that oft-used echoey/loud fashion that lets you know he's a bad ass. From here on in the film veers into the tale of a man who makes a pact with this creature to insure that he marries a beautiful woman and stays young forever. Sadly, there is a price to pay and he must sacrifice maidens to the lustful entity.

What makes **PYASA SHAITAN** a must-see film is that Joginder doesn't just re-edit an older horror film, he re-shapes it. You know something is up when the film stock doesn't match *at all*, and features other chaotic elements. There are solarized flashes of the demon boasting and preening in distorted close-ups, cheap animated lighting and dancing skeletons, and laser beams flying from the eyes of the possessed. On more than one occasion

6 The monsters that appear in these and other films could possibly be related to a *Rakshasha* (राक्षस:) which is a demon or unrighteous spirit in Hindu mythology. Fans of the 70s TV show "The Night Stalker" may remember when one of these critters showed up in the Jimmy Sangster penned episode "Horror in the Heights". *Rakshasas* come in a variety of shapes and sizes since they can change their appearance at will, but one of their main nasty habits is that they feed on both human flesh. They also feast on the fear that they create in the prey they terrorize.

"demons" torment the innocent; these entities are stolen from other films including John Carpenter's **THEY LIVE**, **HALLOWEEN III**, Lon Chaney as **PHANTOM OF THE OPERA**, and TV's "Maxheadroom" flash across the screen. The icing on this psilocin cake are the final few minutes where our demon's plan for his minion is foiled and both of them are sent to hell. Then we are presented with "Coming Soon **PYASA SHAITAN PART II**"! I am *still* waiting.

After an experience like **PYASA SHAITAN** with its jaw-dropping irrationality, Jitendra Chawda's **DAFAN** (2001) and its story of a demon cracking the skulls of men seems a little tame. The film opens with our young heroine, Pooja, having a terrifying nightmare wherein a hideous rubber-faced beast kills a rapist. Pooja confides in Vicky, a police officer that she is in love with, about the attacks and in the end it appears that she is in fact the vengeance-seeking entity. By the end of the film she manages to kill off all the male cast members, including Vicky.

The creature in this feature is typical of what can be found in the least imaginative Indian horror films, which I seemed to have bought this time around. The sad-looking apparition is a person clad in baggy black pajamas with a set of store-bought rubber fright gloves and an ill-fitting mask. As silly as this may seem, these were (and still are) films made on a minuscule budget. They were churned out to satisfy an audience hungry for cheap thrills through scantily clad ladies and leering sex-mad goons facing off against the supernatural.

It's all a matter of disbelief. These monsters may be fake-looking, but I doubt that the men who made most of these films really thought they were producing some excellent fright films. Most of the film are all about making a quick buck with the least about of ambition or skill.

Another fine example of this sexploitation horror is summed up neatly with Kanti Shah's **PYAASA HAIWAN** (2003), wherein our huge stomping monster has a bevy of curvy females to plunder. **PYAASA HAIWAN** is the epitome of the sexy monster movie. Here are voluptuous ladies in skimpy lingerie that roll around with men on beds as well as splash about in swimming pools shamelessly. Just the fodder for a lumbering horny monster to prey upon.

Unlike western films, the monster shows up relatively early in **PYAASA HIAWAN**. In fact, the hairy creature pops up prior to the opening credits to thump about in a haunted mansion. To set the tone for the rest of the film, the entity promptly surprises a couple after they have had sex, kills the man in the nearby graveyard and then molests and kills the woman. The remainder of the film is pretty much the same. What is different in this film is that there is actual nudity, as a quick flash of bare breasts make a surprise appearance during a very brief and unsexy scene (the DVD of **PYAASA HAIWAN** lacks the adult "A Certificate" that normally appears at the beginning of horror films, leaving me to believe that this somehow snuck through the usually strict Indian film censorship). The lack of any real cohesion to the plot other than sex, monster, killing, sex, monster, killing, and you would think that this is a roller coaster of a ride. Nope. Unlike the craziness of **PYASA SHAITAN** which kept my attention throughout, there are no wacky special effects other than the camera shaking, loads of colored light a fog machine, and the endless repeating crack and roll of lightning and thunder (that has become some sort of "must have" stock footage since the early 70s). Now consider when this film was made: 2003. **PYAASA HAIWAN** is stuck in some

kind of low-budget 80s hell. This is, for all intents and purpose, guerrilla film making (pun intended). Oh, and for those of you who hate the dance numbers associated with Indian Cinema, **PYASA SHAITAN** *doesn't have any.*

THE CHUDAIL SUB-GENRE

One of the most popular monsters that terrorizes audiences in these films is a witch/ghost called a *chudail*. A *chudail* (चुडेल) or *churel*, as the entity is more commonly known, is a female ghost from Hindu folklore that feeds on the energy of young virile men. She appears in various forms, and depending on the production budget and skill of the director, these are some of the scariest of the Indian horror genre.

PYAASI ATMA (1988, D: Ismail Inamdar and A. K. Mishra; VCD, no subtitles). Low budget but interesting tale of a young city couple who run into some supernatural trouble while on vacation in a rural coastal town. Poltergeist activity, dramatic flashing lights, and strange encounters can only mean one thing: a *chudail/ghost* is involved and possession of the young bride is not far off. The final ten minutes is pretty good, although it does not resemble in any fashion the gore-soaked cover art on the VCD sleeve.

KAFAN (1990, D: Dhireendra Bohra; DVD, English subtitles). A young woman by the name of Neelam is sensitive to the spirit world and can see evil. Four men and an evil yogi sacrifice a woman in an forbidden ritual that would have made them immortal. Instead they create a *chudail* that goes on a killing spree. Neelam becomes possessed by the *chudail* and periodically changes into the monster, sometimes summoning fellow members of the living dead to assist her. Her boyfriend, Chief Inspector of Police Shekar, soon realizes that Neelam is indeed possessed by the ghost and, with the help of a good yogi, confronts the monster at a local disco. Not a bad film. The effects, make-up, and camera work aren't half bad, but it's the soundtrack that is a killer, being a hodgepodge of sound effects and canned music. The most amusing sequence which is "scored" in this method mixes in frantic African singing and drumming with the moaning thumping noise the TARDIS from the TV show "Dr. Who".

CHUDAIL THE WITCH (1997, D: P. Chandra Kumar; VCD, no subtitles). The best film featuring a *chudail*. A handsome tantrik holy man teams up with the wanton daughter of a town elder. The tantrik teaches the woman various ways to absorb sexual energy and how to transform that energy into black magic. She turns the tables on the holy man and kills him, takes possession of his manservant, and then sets out to ensnare young haughty men with life-essence draining sex. Our "witch" is then trapped in a ring of holy fire produced by a band of good yogi, and three nine-inch nails are driven into her skull. Her lifeless body is then encased in a blessed coffin, sealed in an isolated tomb, and her manservant is driven off into the wilderness. That was the first 30-odd minutes of the film. Now this is where the *chudail* comes in.

"Years Later" the tomb is disturbed and the desiccated remains of the witchy woman is uncovered and the body is removed from the underground crypt and placed in the local morgue for examination. The witch's manservant makes his reappearance and sneaks into the hospital to remove the nails from the witch's skull. She returns from the dead as a *chudail* and continues her reign of terror.

What happens next is pretty comparable to Hong Kong horror films from the 80s. Prime examples being **THE RAPE AFTER** and **DEVIL FETUS**, two incredible films which are worth watching if you have a chance. Kumar's handling of the subject matter is naturally different from the Chinese films, culturally speaking. There is no nudity in this print, but I have read that (not unlike Eurocine productions of the 70s and 80s) saucy scenes of naked breasts and full-on lip-to-lip kissing were inserted for the more raucous, off-the-beaten-track movie houses. The gore is not as abundant or icky as in **DEVIL FETUS**, but the mood and sheer creepy craziness is a good comparison.

Director Kumar has made a few other "Grade C" horror films, although he seems to be more famous for **ADIPAPAM** (1988) which is his adult softcore Malayalam language version of the biblical Adam and Eve story. While this softcore material appears on P. Chandra Kumar (or P. Chandrakumar)'s filmographies, neither of the two horror films are there. So, we may be speaking about two directors with the same name. But I kind of doubt it.

PYASI CHUDAIL (1998, D: Rafai; VCD, no subtitles). A rather subtle and good-looking horror film in which a cursed medallion is the cause of all sorts of havoc for a young female museum curator. An evil spirit emerges from the relic and proceeds to possess the body of the young woman. Eventually it becomes clear that what was released from the object was the *chudail* of a village woman who was raped and killed by a group of city men. In a bid to put a stop to the killings, the police officer boyfriend of the young woman consults a yogi. The final confrontation between the avenging ghost and the holy man reminds me of some of the Taiwanese blood and magic films made around the same time.

CHUDAIL No. 1 (1999, D: R. Kumar; VCD, no subtitles). In a failed kidnapping/robbery by a gang of thugs, a rich man is murdered and his daughter is killed. An intense police investigation is undertaken and most of the criminals are arrested. However, this does not stop the appearance of a sexy *chudail* dressed in a white sari, from killing off the rest of the gang. A surprisingly engaging film with a decent soundtrack, good musical interludes, and a grotesque goo-dripping pot-bellied zombie armed with an ax.

CHANDANI BANI CHUDAIL (2001, D: R. Mittal; VCD, no subtitles). A fun loving group of horny young men hang out at a popular park with equally like-minded young women. Thirty odd minutes into the film, after way too much chit-chatting between the groups, one of the young women is kidnapped by four thrill seekers who end up killing the girl after rough (off screen) sex in a van. As to be expected, the death of this innocent woman triggers the appearance of a *chudail*. With every flash of (stock footage) lighting the ghost strikes, appearing as either a rubber-masked monster in a black cloak or a woman in a bloodied white sari. The guilty parties are killed off in a variety of bloody ways. Turns out that the killing is the work of a flesh and blood young woman who has gone insane due of the death of her sister. One of the worse of the batch.

QATIL CHUDAIL (2002, D:Kanti Shah; VCD, no subtitles). Not to be confused with the old 1935 film of he same name which I have yet to see, this **QATIL CHUDAIL** is a sexploitation thriller. A group of tourists end up in a run down mansion haunted by a *chudail*. Some of the crew are killed by the witch-ghost which can appear as a beautiful woman or as a bloated hag. More sex than horror fills this oddball film, which also features Naga tribesmen who randomly show up to molest a woman for five minutes. The film ends rather abruptly as the *chudail* is stabbed by woman wielding Shiva's trident.

CHUDAIL KA BADLA (2006, D: P. Alagar; VCD, no subtitles). A young police woman captures a key figure in a local smuggling ring only to be shot and killed by fellow officer who was in on it from the beginning. And before you know it, her avenging ghost haunts the criminals. A holy man versed in

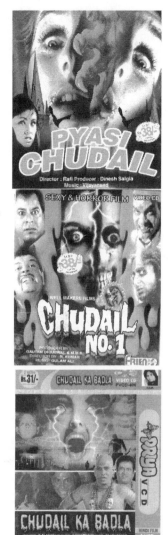

Churel or Chudail films have been popular in Indian horror cinema for almost a century. They are some of the easiest and cheapest horror films to produce. All you need is a spooky ghost or sexy lady in white in a mood for spectral vengeance.

the dark arts is brought in to help our gang of cut-throats as the *chudail* kills them off one by one. As a late entry into the sub-genre, with a slightly higher budget than expected, the film benefits from digital effects and some decent cinematography, but is rather tedious and has a poor soundtrack.

ROOH (2008, D: Sanjay Khandelwal, DVD, so subtitles) One of the newer productions to feature a sexy ghost configured into a *chundail* tale; very glossy but also very dull. The two highlights of the film are the disco-dance numbers performed by ghosts and ghouls in spandex and nagahide.

AN ASSORTMENT OF CRITTERS...

KHOONI MUDAA (1989, D: Mohan Bhakri; VCD, no subtitles). A hideous creature with razor-sharp claws and laser eye-beams is attacking the young men and women of a small college town. The police are baffled (as they are often in these films), and the kids die off in between their sexual exploits and musical numbers. The final fifteen minutes is very thrilling as the demon attacks an entire group of men and women in an old mansion. The monster flies through the air, picking off its prey one by one, ripping out the sinews of its poor victims' arms and legs. It then drags them around the mansion as if they were bloodied, screaming marionettes. Appallingly gruesome for its budget. After a great deal of bloodshed and gore (for this type of film), the monster is finally destroyed when confronted by a yogi. One of the film where I wish it did have subtitles.

"Grade C" Adult Certificate bound productions aren't just horror films full of sex; there are various genres... Similar to the direct-to-TV or web-based do-it-yourself style of present day filmmaking.

Despite the fact that the film is an apparent rip off of Wes Craven's first **NIGHTMARE ON ELM STREET** film, you may recall that Freddy was in part inspired by a Hindu demon known as a *Vetala* (वेताल), or possibly a *Rakshasha* who have long razor-sharp fingernails and have been reported to attack people in their dreams/sleep[7]. So, you can say, the film has actually come full circle. At least in this film the demon is grotesque looking and not some store-bought Halloween costume.

The better known **NIGHTMARE ON ELM STREET** rip-off from India is Shyam and Tulsi Ramsay's 1993 **MAHAKAAL**. But between the two, and

7 A good jumping off point for understanding the incredible variety and cultural importance of demons and monsters is David D. Gilmore's book "Monsters: Evil Beings, Mythical Beasts, and All Manner of Imaginary Terrors", University of Pennsylvania Press, 2002 - 210 pages.

A rarity in 90s Indian horror: the ooy-gooey reanimated corpse from **PURANI KABRA**

despite the Ramsay's film having more of a budget, this film has a better monster... even with the creature's laser eye beams and animated atomic breath.

PURANI KABRA (1998, D: K. I. Sheikh; VCD, no subtitles). What essentially begins as a pretty lame action/comedy/sexploitation romp with supernatural overtones soon develops into a pretty fun horror film. Director K.I. Sheikh has made quite a few sexy/action and sexy/horror films, and **PURANI KABRA** rates as his best. A film crew arrives at a remote town where they proceed to film a sexy musical. In the meantime the local criminals murder people and menace the film crew. If you make it through the first 30 minutes you're treated to a pretty cool goo-dripping, acid-spitting zombie/swami that kills off the most annoying characters for the remaining 90 minutes. Another bonus is the amazing amount of attractive cleavage in this film.

BHOOT KA DARR (1999, D: S. Gawli; VCD, no subtitles). Store bought Halloween props and other bargain-basement goodies populate this meager horror effort. A group of female friends contact a spooky yogi in an attempt to stop an evil force from tormenting them. Basically a sexploitation film with sassy ladies battling various horny men, rubber-masked demons, that annoying stock footage lightning, all the while participating in badly choreographed booty and boobs dance numbers. The film's opening credits boasts of the talents of some really bad professional impersonators of top Bollywood talents Shahrukh Khan, Anil Kapoor, Dev Anand and Amitabh Bachhan. Simply awful. Just when things look dire for the last remaining female, the god Shiva grants her the use of his trident and the pesky demon causing all her problems is easily dispatched.

SADU AUR SHAITAN (1999?, D: Kareem/Karim; VCD, no subtitles). Although slow moving, **SADU AUR SHAITAN** is a fascinating and ultimately satisfying tale of a holy girl child born to a humble couple and the assorted swami and yogi out to kill her. Apparently, she's something special and the old men aren't too keen on having her live to adulthood. No monsters pop up in this supernatural tale of professional jealousy, but there is a lot of religious magic and power involved when it is revealed that she may be a reincarnation of a goddess. A fairly serious effort with precious few comedic sequences and only one subdued traditional musical number.

SHAITAN TANTRIX (1999, D: Wajid Sheikh; VCD, so subtitles). The film opens with a ridiculous disco-dance sequence (and they don't get any better as the film progresses) which sets the mood for the rest of this sexy/martial arts/action thriller with supernatural overtones. An evil-minded tantrik holy man, quite possibly a Yogini who worships Bhairavi (the fiercest aspect of Mother Divine/Shaktai), is determined to acquire immense power through summoning demons to do his bidding. One demon (which looks a sexy lady in a striped bikini, thus saving the producer some cash) sets about causing mischief and cracking some skulls.

BHOOTON KA HONEYMOON (2001, D: Ashok Jamuar; VCD, no subtitles). Forget it. Horrible Scooby Doo of a film. Seriously, the worst of the batch. Everything sucks about this film and there is nothing redeemable about it. Period. Thank Kali it only cost me $1.50.

SHAITANI DRACULA (2006, D: Harinam Singh; VCD, no subtitles). Clocking in at a short and very sweet 80 minutes, **SHAITANI DRACULA** is an incredible piece of filmmaking. A chubby, very talkative, moustached Dracula in a black cowboy hat boasts about his blood lust through a mouthful of store-bought plastic vampire teeth. In between some very lame softcore sex and awful musical numbers, we are presented with flying vampire ladies in skimpy white outfits with large cardboard wings who glide after their horrified victims. There are, of course, the more commonly found motifs you just can't live without: rubber masked monsters, men in skeleton pajamas, and the ubiquitous lighting crash. The final epic battle between the King of All Vampires and one feisty woman armed with a wooden cross is the clincher. Probably the closest this genre has come to producing a modern day Dada/Outsider masterpiece. *Watch at your own risk.*

POST-MORTEM:

What you just read pretty much sums up what you can expect when plunking down a large wad of cash for movies you know nothing about. Although I may have complained about a lot of the films, I am glad I sat through their torment . The major appeal that these films have for me is their sheer exotic quality. As I scour the internet I keep on discovering additional thrills... or what *appears* to be a possible gem, because you just don't know what they're like until you watch them. In some ways, my randomly buying VCDs and DVDs is not unlike peeling an onion and each layer leads me to a new slew of bizarro horror/monster, movies from India, Thailand, Malaysia, The Philippines, Taiwan, Turkey, and other countries. In another way, it drives me up the wall knowing that what I do find on the web is just the tip of a vast cinematic iceberg. I am sure that there are hundreds of more fantastic films that have yet to be released on VCD, or if they have, they are sitting on a dusty shelf at a store in a country I'll probably never visit.

THE DISCLAIMER: *As an outsider who doesn't claim anything other than a giddy zeal over watching these Indian horror films, I will be the first to say that I am no scholar. I welcome any corrections, additions and/or criticism.*

LOVING GODDESS OR WRATHFUL DEITY?
Very Brief Overview on how some Hindu Gods are perceived in Indian Horror Cinema

Just what is that six-armed, toothy, fierce female idol that those heathen Indians worship? She has fangs, she's sticking her tongue out, there are skulls and a severed head in one of her many hands. What kind of blood-thirsty creature is this? Most Western audiences have that twisted and sorely misunderstood view of Kali, one of the wrathful aspect of the Hindu goddess Durga. Her terrifying appearance usually conjures up images of devils and evil. Films like **INDIANA JONES AND THE TEMPLE OF DOOM** didn't help. Shaktai, Durga, Kali, and other angry goddesses are just as complicated and unfathomable at times as their human female counterparts.

In Western horror films, and especially those that deal with witchcraft and the supernatural, the idea of evil is usually sourced to Satan, Lucifer or the Devil. Our horror cinema is based on this very Judeo-Christian, black and white world of evil. In Indian cinema evil is typically a human trait (even Indian demons aren't necessarily bad). Such maligned power is bestowed to an Indian witch or warlock as the result of their devout worship of a particular Hindu deity. The relationship between a god and its devotee is a complicated one, and will be glossed over rather quickly for this brief essay.

Most of the films I've covered are West Bengali in origin, an Indian state where even to this day there are said to be many active *Tantriks* or holy men. In these low-budget movies, pseudo-legends are often adapted using idioms from the folk theatre. There are good *tantriks* that help folks with daily rituals, and then there are those bad ones who performs vile deeds through *tantrik* mantras or black magic and mantras of *shudra devatas*. These mantras are a method of channelling the power of a chosen god or goddess; the Hindu pantheon is full of deities that pretty much give anyone power if they ask for it. These beings are not evil per say, they are pretty neutral. The power they impart is indiscriminate.

In these films our protagonists typically call upon what appear to be demonic-looking goddesses (although there have been a few movies where Shiva is invoked, but mostly it's a goddess). Hindu deities aren't so black and white as their western cousins. For example, while the Loving Mother Goddess, Durga, is the most matriarchal of all the gods, she, like the other gods, has many aspects and incarnations. For the most part she is perceived as a beneficial goddess, but she has an angry side; she is very, very powerful as both a giver of life and a destroyer of worlds. Durga can manifest as Kali the destroyer and other dark forms.

Whereas Durga/Kali appears in many films, the most popular "wrathful" go-to goddess in these horror films is Patala Bhairavi (the prefix "patal" means underworld or netherworld, hence most of the cinematic temples for this fearful goddess are in graveyards, caves or underground). She is an incarnation of Goddess Shakti, which is the ultimate female form of everything – the divine feminine. She is the very ancient primal goddess of the Hindu mythology, and is

PATALA BHAIRAVI

more of a concept of the ultimate divine feminine power from which other goddess probably sprang forth. You don't want to mess with her! Frightening statues of this goddess appears in **SHAITAN TANTRIX, KAFAN,** and others. The form of Bhairavi The Wrathful is often depicted as a fanged, dark-skinned wild crone, armed with weapons and draped in gore, quit the shocking image of a loving mother goddess that is otherwise a beautiful woman.

In conclusion, to fall back on an old adage, you can't judge a book by it cover. Or in this case by how an armful of horror-oriented genre films from a culture you may know little about could very well color your option of one's deities.

~ Tim Paxton
with Cara Romano